75

Duane Kolbe

S0-DHX-434

OUR NATION GROWS UP

Westward the course of empire takes its way

OUR
NATION GROWS UP

BY

EUGENE C. BARKER
HEAD OF THE DEPARTMENT OF HISTORY
UNIVERSITY OF TEXAS

WILLIAM E. DODD
HEAD OF THE DEPARTMENT OF HISTORY
THE UNIVERSITY OF CHICAGO

WALTER P. WEBB
PROFESSOR OF HISTORY
UNIVERSITY OF TEXAS

ROW, PETERSON AND COMPANY
EVANSTON, ILLINOIS

NEW YORK   SAN FRANCISCO

COPYRIGHT, 1932, 1938
BY
Row, Peterson and Company
1740

MANUFACTURED IN THE UNITED STATES OF AMERICA

PURPOSE AND PLAN OF THE BOOK

Our Nation Grows Up conforms closely in content and style to Chapters XI–XXVII of *The Story of Our Nation*. The text has been carefully revised, however, and additional units and chapters have been inserted where more material seemed most desirable.

The authors have used outstanding personalities and intrinsically dramatic movements to carry the story, but their unvarying purpose has been to present the thread of the narrative as a continuous, unified whole. They believe that even very young children can be trained in the rudiments of orderly thinking.

The book is not, therefore, a compilation of disconnected biographical sketches and picturesque episodes. It is the story of the making of our nation, in simple and concrete language adapted to the comprehension and the interest of young readers. It is a history.

For the sake of vividness, much of the narrative is paraphrased, from original reports and diaries. The words of the quotations have sometimes been freely adapted to the vocabulary of young readers, but the meaning and much of the style of the originals are faithfully preserved.

The text of the 1938 edition of *Our Nation Grows Up* has been brought up to date. Several new illustrations have been substituted which tell the story more ably. The activities have been entirely rewritten. Suggestions for supplementary reading have been placed at the end of each unit preview.

CONTENTS

Unit One
THE NEW NATION IS BORN

Unit Two
THE NATION LEARNS TO STAND ALONE

Unit Three
THE NATION EXPANDS TO THE PACIFIC

UNIT ONE

THE NEW NATION IS BORN

When we look at the map of the United States today we see the home of one of the largest nations in the world. This home land is bounded by the Atlantic Ocean on the east and by the Pacific on the west. It extends from Canada in the north to Mexico in the south. It contains forty-eight states and more than a hundred and twenty million people.

In spite of its large size and its great number of inhabitants, the United States is a young nation. Just a little more than a hundred and fifty years ago it gained its independence from England. At first it had only thirteen states. Its territory ended at the Mississippi River instead of the Pacific Ocean. It then had fewer than four million people.

The old, old nations of Europe paid very little attention to the new country. They could not imagine that it would ever be strong enough to play an important part in the affairs of the world. It is not strange that they thought so poorly of the United States, for many of our own people thought that it might be better to break up the Union and let each state remain a separate country.

How, then, did our nation grow from such a weak beginning to its present strength and importance? The stories in this book will help us to answer that interesting question.

We shall learn first how a little group of men from the different states got together and planned our government. General Washington, who had done so much to free the United States from the rule of England, became the first President and set the new government going. Like the captain of a ship, he steered the nation on its course.

After eight years as President, Washington returned to his plantation in Virginia, and John Adams became captain of the ship of state. He followed the course that Washington had set.

Thomas Jefferson, the author of the Declaration of Independence, was the third President. His most important gift to the greatness of the United States was the buying of the territory between the Mississippi River and the Rocky Mountains. By this purchase he doubled the size of the United States.

STORIES TO READ FOR UNIT ONE

Coe, F. E., *Makers of the Nation* (American Book Company).

Tappan, E. M., *American Hero Stories* (Houghton, Mifflin Company).

Burton, A. H., *Four American Patriots* (American Book Company).

Foote, A. E., and Skinner, A. W., *Makers and Defenders of America* (American Book Company).

Faris, J. T., *Makers of Our History* (Ginn and Company).

McMurray, C. A., *Pioneers of the Rocky Mountains and the West* (The Macmillan Company).

OUR NATION GROWS UP

Chapter I

THE INDEPENDENCE OF THE UNITED STATES

George and Martha Washington

When there was no United States. We call our nation the United States of America. Today it is one of the largest and strongest nations in the world, but only a little more than a hundred and fifty years ago there was no United States. We shall learn in this book how the United States began as an independent nation, and how it became strong and great.

The English colonies in America. The United States grew out of a quarrel between England and its thirteen American colonies. Perhaps you remember the names of the colonies. They were New Hampshire, Massachusetts, Connecticut, Rhode Island, New York, New

Jersey, Pennsylvania, Delaware, Maryland, Virginia, North Carolina, South Carolina, and Georgia.

The quarrel between England and the colonies. For many, many years the people in the colonies were happy under the rule of England. Although they lived in America, they thought of themselves as Englishmen and were proud of England's greatness.

A time came, however, when the colonists began to believe that England was treating them unfairly. The government passed a law saying that the Americans must pay a tax. The colonists disobeyed the law and refused to pay the tax, because they believed that the government had no right to take their money without their consent.

This was the beginning of the quarrel. It lasted for about ten years. England sent soldiers to America to try to make the colonists pay the tax, but they still refused to pay and the quarrel went on and on. At last the soldiers and the colonists came to blows. The first battle was fought at Lexington, in Massachusetts, in April, 1775.

The Declaration of Independence. Soon after the battle of Lexington a number of men from the different colonies met at Philadelphia to decide what the Americans should do. The meeting was called the Continental Congress.

The members of the Congress tried for nearly a year to make peace with England, but the war went on. Finally they gave up the effort to make peace and declared the colonies independent. The Declaration of Independence was written by Thomas Jefferson, a member of the Continental Congress from Virginia. It said that the colonists had decided to separate from England and start a new nation of their own. You see, now, how the United States grew out of the quarrel between England and its thirteen American colonies.

The War for Independence. England was unwilling to give up its colonies and tried to keep them by force. The War for Independence lasted nearly seven years. General George Washington commanded the American armies and led them to victory. In 1783 England made peace and agreed to recognize the United States as a free and independent nation.

For his services in winning the independence of the United States, Washington is called the "Father of our country." But his important services were not ended by peace. In the next chapter we shall see how he became the first President of the United States, and helped to start the government of the new nation.

Washington at Mount Vernon, a painting by Chappel

Chapter II

MAKING A GOVERNMENT FOR THE NEW NATION

James Madison

OUR GOVERNMENT TODAY

Our government at work. We can best understand the government of the new nation, if we look to the city of Washington and study the government of today.

We may well feel proud of Washington, one of the most beautiful cities in the world. There the nation's government is carried on in many fine buildings.

The largest and finest building, one that rises above all the others, is the Capitol. Its dome towers nearly three hundred feet in the air. At night it shines with hundreds of lights and may be seen for miles around. The Capitol is the center of the city of Washington; it is the center of the government of our country.

(4)

The Capitol at Washington. Within this great building of stone and marble the laws of the nation are made.

Around the Capitol are grouped the magnificent Library of Congress and splendid buildings containing offices for the senators and members of Congress. A broad avenue leads from the Capitol to the White House where the President lives. Not far from the White House are the Treasury building, the War and

Navy building, and other great government offices.

But it is inside the Capitol building that the visitor to Washington finds the greatest interest. In the right wing is the Senate chamber where ninety-six men meet to do their part in passing laws for nearly a hundred and thirty million people. There are two senators from each of the forty-eight states.

Opposite the Senate, in the left wing of the Capitol, is the House of Representatives. This room is much larger than the Senate chamber. More than four hundred members meet there. The number of members from the various states differs. The states where there are a great many people send many members, and the thinly settled states send few. But every state, no matter how few people it has, sends at least one member.

The Senate and House together form our Congress. Congress makes laws for the whole nation.

The White House is the home of the President and his family, and there the President has his office. The visitor to Washington does not often get to see the President because he is such a busy man. He is surrounded by clerks and secretaries, and is guarded by special police officers, some of whom are in uniform and some in plain clothes. The President is busy because senators and members of Congress, governors from the various states, and business men and politicians from everywhere are constantly trying to see and talk with him.

The President is the first man of the nation, the head of the government. It is his business to advise Congress, and to see that all the laws are obeyed.

The Supreme Court, or highest court, is the head of the third important branch of the United States government. The Court occupies a beautiful building of dignified white marble. Many rows of tall columns form the portico or porch. Nine judges make up the court, and the visitor will be greatly impressed by the solemn dignity and importance of the judges.

The judges hold their office for life. When they appear in court they wear long black robes and sit in high seats. It is the business of the Supreme Court and of a number of lower courts to settle disputes that arise over the meaning of laws that have been passed by Congress and signed by the President.

Congress makes the laws. It is the duty of the President to enforce the laws. And if disputes come up about the meaning of the laws, the Supreme Court settles the disputes. The visitor who goes to Washington during the winter months can see all these officers at work.

But how did we come to have such a government, made up of a Congress, a President, and a Supreme Court? To answer this question we must go back to the War for Independence.

HOW OUR GOVERNMENT WAS MADE

The Union in danger. When the thirteen colonies declared their independence and separated from England, they needed some sort of government to keep them united and help them to work together. So long as the war was going on they looked to the Continental Congress for orders and advice, but after the war was over, the different states paid less and less attention to the Continental Congress.

It looked as if the Union were going to break up and each state form a separate nation. How could such a misfortune be prevented? Hoping to solve the problem and save the Union, the people again decided to send men to a meeting at Philadelphia. When they got together they could talk things over and see what could be done.

The Federal Convention tries to save the Union. This meeting was held at the old State House in Philadelphia. The building is still standing, and the room in which the members met is kept just as it was when the meeting was going on. The meeting is called the Federal Convention. It met about the middle of May, 1787, and was in session four months, until the middle of September.

Each state sent its greatest and wisest men to the Philadelphia meeting. There was George Washington who had come from his home in Virginia. He was made president, or chairman, of the Convention. There was Benjamin Franklin from Pennsylvania. He was now eighty-one years old, but his mind was still bright and his head full of wisdom and common sense.

There were two young men whom we have not met before. Alexander Hamilton came from New York and James Madison from Virginia.

Alexander Hamilton was born in the English West Indies in 1757, and when the Convention met he was thirty years old. As a boy he was fond of study and gave promise of growing up to be a brilliant man.

To plan the government for a whole new nation was no easy task
for the delegates to the Federal Convention.

When he was fifteen years old he was sent to New
York City, where he became a student in King's College, now Columbia University. Though he was only
eighteen years old when the war with England began,
he formed a company, drilled it and, for a time, led it
in battle.

Hamilton's ability was soon noticed by Washington,
who transferred him to his own headquarters. During
all the rest of the war Hamilton was Washington's
most trusted assistant, taking care of his secret papers
and copying and sending out to the different officers
Washington's most important orders.

After the war Hamilton settled in New York City, studied law, and became one of the great lawyers of New York. He always took a keen interest in public affairs, and was a leader in New York politics.

Hamilton wanted a strong government to hold the states together. In fact, Hamilton would have been glad to see the United States turned into a kingdom with George Washington on the throne. He rather liked kings, if they were good ones, because they could rule with a strong hand and make the people obey.

James Madison, next to Washington, was Hamilton's closest friend in the Federal Convention. He was born in Virginia, in 1751, and was therefore six years older than Hamilton. He was a graduate of Princeton College, in New Jersey. He had neither the cold, dignified manner of Washington nor the proud and haughty appearance of Hamilton. He was a small man whom you would not turn to look at as you would at Washington or Hamilton. But Madison was one of the most important men at the Convention. There were three reasons why he was important.

First, Madison knew more about government than any one else who was there. He knew how governments were made, and how they worked.

Second, he went to the Convention with a definite plan of government already written out. He knew what was needed to hold the states together and prevent the Union from breaking up. The plan of government that he had drawn up was taken by members of the convention as a model for the new government which they framed.

Third, he kept the most careful record of what went on in the Convention. Each day he took his seat where he could see and hear everything, and he made notes all the time. From Madison's notes we get most of our information about what went on. .

For these three reasons, this quiet, retiring little man with his plan, his notebooks, and his great knowledge of history is called the "Father of the Constitution"; that is, the man who had most to do with making our government what it is today. Twenty-one years after the Convention finished its work he became the fourth President of the United States.

How did the Convention go about its work? If you had been living in Philadelphia at the time, you could not have found out, because each day when the Convention met, the doors were closed and no one was permitted to know what went on behind those doors. Every man was pledged to keep secret what was said and done there.

Day after day passed and weeks grew into months, and still the people did not know what was going on. Even the newspaper reporters could not find out. Some people were certain that the able men in the Convention would make a good, strong government; others felt less certain and shook their heads in doubt.

The Convention makes the Constitution. At last, on the seventeenth of September, the work was finished, and the people waited anxiously to hear what had been done. All that the members had to show for their four months of work was a paper which they had written. It was not a long paper either, not longer

Delegates from various states signing the Constitution

than twelve or fifteen pages of this book, but it proved
to be the most important paper, with the exception of
the Declaration of Independence, that was ever written
in the United States. It was the complete plan for the
government that we have already seen at work in
Washington. It was the Constitution of the United
States of America.

The first sentence of the Constitution reads, "We
the People of the United States . . . do establish this
Constitution for the United States of America." That
is a remarkable sentence. It means that the people
of the United States make their own government, that
they govern themselves.

When the Convention ended its work, all the members returned home to explain what they had done,
and to urge the people to approve the Constitution.

Washington receiving the delegates from Congress who came to Mt. Vernon to tell him of his election as first President of the new nation.

They carried copies of the Constitution with them and distributed them among the people. The new plan of government would not be carried out, until the people of at least nine states had agreed to it.

There must have been great excitement when a member returning from the Convention stopped at a tavern or inn for the night. Word went around that there was a man from Philadelphia who had been working on the new plan of government and could tell the people what it was like. The people asked him all sorts of questions about it and the traveler explained again and again what had been done.

He told them the Federal Convention voted that the head of the government was to be the President.

What was the President to be like, someone asked,— a king?

No, he would not be like a king. Kings were born to their office, and held their office for life whether the people liked them or not. The President was to be chosen by the people, and would serve for only four years, but he might then be reëlected if the people wanted him as President for another four years.

What had they decided to do with the old Continental Congress? Would it be continued?

No, there would be a new Congress, made up of a Senate and a House of Representatives. This Congress would make the laws.

There would be a Supreme Court to settle disputes about the laws.

If the people approved the Constitution, an election would be held in November to choose the President and the members of Congress. The President would appoint the judges who made up the courts.

Then the traveler might read parts of the Constitution to show what had been done.

The Union is saved. But would nine states approve the Constitution? All sorts of objections were raised to the new plan of government. Men gathered in the taverns and village stores to debate and argue about every part of the plan. Everywhere the members of the Convention were urging the people to accept.

Washington wrote letters day and night to his friends in Virginia, urging them to accept the Constitution.

Hamilton and Madison wrote nearly a hundred articles, explaining the meaning of every part of the Constitution. They begged the people to accept it and give it a trial. They pointed out that if it did not work well it could be changed. These articles were first published in the newspapers, but were later collected and published in a book called _The Federalist_.

Nearly a year passed before the suspense ended, but before the end of 1788 eleven states had accepted the Constitution, and the plan for a strong, new government could be tried. The other two states, North Carolina and Rhode Island, approved it later, and the Union of the thirteen states was saved.

The Union was now much stronger than it had ever been before, even stronger than it had been during the war with England. The Constitution gave the new government power to collect taxes and raise money to pay running expenses. It could keep up an army and navy. It could control trading with foreign countries and could make foreign governments treat American citizens fairly. And it could force people in the states to obey its laws.

Washington heads the new government. To start the new government, all eyes looked to Washington. Would he accept the office of President? He did not want it. He enjoyed his home life at Mount Vernon, and was interested in managing his plantations. But his mail was heavy with letters begging him to take the presidency and put the new government on its feet. Not only the friends of the Constitution but those also who opposed it wanted him, because everybody trusted

Mount Vernon, home of the first President.

his honor, his ability, and his love for his country. They knew that if it was possible to make the new government a success, he would do it.

As soon as Washington was convinced that he was really needed, he said that he would serve, if elected. That was enough. He received every vote cast. No other President has ever been elected without even one opposing vote.

A SHORT STORY TO TELL

When the war with England was over, the Americans needed a government to keep the thirteen states united in one strong union instead of dividing into thirteen weak little countries. The greatest men of the whole country met at Philadelphia and worked out a plan for such a government. Washington was chairman of the Convention; but James Madison had more to do with the making of the plan of government than anybody else.

The plan of government was called the Constitution. It was made for thirteen states with less than four million people in them, but we are still using it for our union of forty-eight states and nearly a hundred and thirty million people.

The home of our government is in the splendid city of Washington. Thousands and thousands of men and women work for the government all over the country, but at the head of the government in Washington are the President, Congress, and the Supreme Court.

WHY?

1. Why was there a need for a government to be planned?

2. Why was Madison one of the most important men at the Federal Convention?

3. Why did it take nearly a year to have the Constitution accepted?

4. Why was Washington a good choice for the first president?

WHO?

5. Who was called the "Father of Our Country"?

6. Who was called the "Father of the Constitution"?

7. Who wrote "The Federalist"?

8. Who made the laws under the new Government?

9. Who was to settle disputes about the laws?

Chapter III

WASHINGTON SETS THE NEW GOVERNMENT GOING

Alexander Hamilton

WASHINGTON TAKES CHARGE

Washington, the first President of the United States. It was planned to begin the new government in March, 1789. But there were no railroads, automobiles, or airplanes in those days, and people could not always get to places on time. During the winter of 1789 the weather was so bad and the mud and snow were so deep that the members of Congress were a month late in getting to New York City. Here the new government was to be started, for the Capitol was not yet built at Washington, nor was the city of Washington even started.

(18)

When the members of Congress arrived in New York, they had to count the votes for President and Vice-President. Everybody knew that Washington was elected President and that John Adams of Massachusetts was Vice-President. But Congress had to go through the form, the red tape, of counting the votes and telling them of their election.

When the committee of Congress arrived at Mount Vernon to tell Washington of his election, he started at once for New York. He knew that Congress could do nothing until he got there, and he did not want to cause the members of Congress to wait for him.

Washington would have preferred to stay at home, looking after his plantations, and spending the rest of his life in a quiet way. But he was never a man to shirk a duty. When he was only twenty we saw him carrying Governor Dinwiddie's message warning the French to get out of the Ohio Valley. Two years later we saw him in a hail of bullets trying to save General Braddock's army from destruction by the French and their Indian warriors. At the age of forty-two he took command of the American army, and under his command it won the independence of the United States. He helped to make the new government.

He was now fifty-seven years old, and the people were calling him to set the new government on its feet and start it going. No other man in America could have done this difficult task so well.

Though it was a hard trip to New York, it must have been a pleasant one, for every step of Washington's journey was like the march of a much-loved

Everywhere Washington was warmly greeted on his way from
Mt. Vernon to New York to take up his duties as President.

hero. First, his neighbors and close friends met him
at Alexandria, Virginia, to say good-bye and tell him
of their trust and good wishes. They thought that he
would lead the new government wisely and safely. As
he went on, people met him at every town. Officers
who had been with him in the army came to shake his
hand. Military companies went with him from town
to town. There were banquets, speeches, toasts, and
fireworks. Children spread flowers in his path.

Washington would have been dull indeed if he had
not known long before he reached New York that the
people admired and trusted him.

On April 30, 1789, Washington took up his duties as first President of the United States.

Washington's problems. The new government had two difficult tasks, or problems. The first task was to get money to pay the old debts which had piled up during the war with England, and to pay the men who worked for the government. The second task was to make foreign countries treat the United States as an equal; to get them to allow our citizens the same rights that we allowed theirs.

Washington forms his cabinet. To help him with the money problem, Washington appointed Alexander Hamilton to be Secretary of the Treasury. To help him with foreign countries, he appointed Thomas Jef-

LaFayette, the friend of Washington and friend to the American people, visits Washington at Mt. Vernon.

ferson to be Secretary of Foreign Affairs. To help in managing the army and navy, he appointed General Henry Knox, one of his old generals, to be Secretary of War. And to advise him in matters of law, he appointed his friend and neighbor, Governor Edmund Randolph of Virginia, to be Attorney-General.

Each of these officers was at the head of a great department of government, and together they formed the President's cabinet, his group of advisers. The President talked with them about all important matters of government.

THE SETTLEMENT OF THE MONEY PROBLEM

Hamilton sees two ways to raise money. Hamilton's first task was to get money. Besides needing money for running expenses, to pay the salaries of officers and members of Congress, the government owed nearly seventy-five million dollars. This debt must be paid, but how? There were two ways for the government to get money. One way was to collect taxes; the other was to borrow. Hamilton decided to use both ways.

But paying taxes is always unpleasant. People know that they must have a government; they know that they must have laws to protect themselves and their property; and they know that men must be paid to carry on the government. They know that it costs money to run the government and do all these things. But still they do not like to pay taxes.

Hamilton gives his taxes a "sugar-coating." Hamilton knew very well that the people would not want to pay taxes. He tried therefore to collect money for the government without letting the people know that they were paying it.

To bring about this magic effect, Hamilton asked Congress to pass a law putting a tax on goods brought into the United States from foreign countries. The merchants who brought in the goods would then pay the tax and add the same amount to the price at which they would sell the goods. The merchants would get their money back from the people who bought the goods, but very few of the people who bought from the merchants would realize that they were paying a tax to the government. They would think that they were paying simply the price of the goods.

A law to carry out this part of Hamilton's plan was one of the first acts passed by the Congress of the new government. It was introduced by Hamilton's old friend, James Madison of Virginia, who was a member of the first Congress under the new government.

Hamilton borrows money for the United States. The second part of Hamilton's plan for raising money was to borrow. He had no difficulty in borrowing as soon as people saw that the government was strong enough to get money by taxes. They knew then that the government could and would pay back the money that it borrowed from them. The government paid them interest for the use of their money, and they considered the loan a good investment, a good way to make their money grow.

With the money which he got through taxing and borrowing, Hamilton paid off the old debts; and the new government was able to start with a good name for paying its debts.

THE SETTLEMENT OF TROUBLES WITH EUROPE

Washington settles our troubles with England. In the Peace Treaty of 1783, England agreed to the independence of the United States. But so long as our old, weak government lasted, it would not treat the United States as a free country. It would not let American merchants and shipowners trade in England on the same fair terms that our government allowed English merchants and shipowners to trade in the United States. When Washington became President, however, England agreed to treat our people as the United States treated Englishmen.

Washington settles our troubles with Spain. Spain, like England, knew that the old government of the United States had been rather weak. So Spain tried to take nearly all the territory now included in Alabama and Mississippi. It tried to keep people in Kentucky, Tennessee, and Ohio from sending goods down the Mississippi River in boats, saying that the river belonged to Spain. This was an important matter to the western settlers, because they had no other way to ship their goods to market.

After Washington took charge of the government, Spain gave up its claim to our territory and no longer tried to keep American settlers and traders from using the Mississippi River.

Washington has trouble with France. Three years after Washington became President, France got into a war with all the European countries around it. It needed help against so many enemies, and turned naturally to the United States.

The French people had helped the Americans against King George; now, they said, the United States must help France.

But Washington declared that the United States could not afford to go into another war. It wanted to be friends with all countries. Therefore he issued a message saying that the United States would not take sides in the war between France and its enemies.

The French people were greatly disappointed and very angry because of Washington's refusal to help them. All during the rest of Washington's presidency and that of John Adams, who followed him, France was on the point of war against the United States. Fortunately the quarrel was finally settled without war.

WASHINGTON'S SERVICES

The father of his country. We can now understand why Washington is called the "Father of his Country."

He led the armies which won from England the independence of the United States.

He headed the convention that made the new government under which the United States has grown great and well respected. The Constitution that Washington helped make at Philadelphia in 1787 is still the rule-book of our government. It tells officers how to govern.

As President, Washington headed the new government for eight years and set it to running smoothly. It seemed that every time the country was in danger or

needed a wise leader to keep it out of trouble, all eyes
turned to Washington. He was indeed "first in war, first
in peace, and first in the hearts of his countrymen."

But even Washington did not escape criticism. A
new political party began to grow up while he was
President, and Washington said that some of the men
in this party abused him as if he were a pickpocket.

When his second term as head of the new government ended, however, the people would have elected
him for a third term, but Washington refused. He was
becoming an old man. He wanted to go back to his
beautiful Mount Vernon home and rest. Besides, he
knew that the new government was now working well,
and he believed that it would set a bad example for
one man to hold the presidency for a longer time than
eight years. Kings ruled for life, but a president should
rule for only a short time and then turn over the office
to some one else.

So, on the fourth of March, 1797, Washington
turned his face homeward. His work was done. Others
must now take up the tasks that he laid down, and carry
them on. He died at Mount Vernon, two years later.

John Adams follows Washington as second President.
Virginia and Massachusetts had taken the lead in the
quarrel with England. The War for Independence began in Massachusetts and ended in Virginia. Washington, the greatest of all Virginians, became the first
President. It was fitting that the second President
should come from Massachusetts. So John Adams was
elected to follow Washington. He had held many
public offices. He had helped Jefferson write the

Declaration of Independence. He had helped Benjamin Franklin and John Jay to make peace with England when the War for Independence was ended. He had been Vice-President during all Washington's eight years as President. Now he was to be president.

John Adams

Adams tried to carry on the government in the way that Washington had started it; and the country continued to grow strong.

A SHORT STORY TO TELL

When the new plan of government was accepted, all eyes turned toward George Washington. The people chose him to be the first President, and he took the oath of office in 1789. He was elected again at the end of four years and so held the office for eight years.

Washington had two very important tasks to perform. The first task was to get money enough to pay the old debts of the government, and the second was to get the governments and people of European countries to treat the United States and its people properly.

Washington chose Alexander Hamilton to help him with the money problem, and Hamilton was very successful in getting money to pay the old debts and to pay the expenses of the new government.

Washington chose Thomas Jefferson to help him

in dealing with foreign governments, and Jefferson, too, was successful, though not quite so successful as Hamilton had been.

Washington refused to hold the office of President for more than eight years, and so far our other Presidents have followed his example. Nobody has ever been President longer than eight years.

John Adams was elected to carry on the government when Washington refused to serve a third term.

WORDS AND MEANINGS

1. Be able to pronounce each of the following words then read the group of words that tells its meaning.

cabinet	a law
shirk	finding fault
act	to get out of doing work
investment	a group of citizens who have the same idea about government
criticism	advisers chosen by the president
red tape	money paid by the people for the support of the government
political party	a way to make money grow
taxes	too much attention to small, unimportant matters

2. Write sentences using the words above. Have your sentences tell something about the money problem that Washington had to face.

3. Explain how Washington tried to gain the respect of foreign countries.

Chapter IV

JEFFERSON OPENS THE WAY
TO THE FAR WEST

Thomas Jefferson

PRESIDENT JEFFERSON BUYS LOUISIANA

The western boundary of the United States. The United
States has not always been as large as it is now. When
the War for Independence ended, it extended on the
west no farther than the Mississippi River. First Spain
and then France owned the land west of the great river.
Spain owned also a narrow strip of territory along
the northern shore of the Gulf of Mexico. So the
United States, as you see, did not own even one bank
of the river as far as its mouth.

Why the United States needed the Mississippi River.
The Mississippi River became very important to the

settlers in Kentucky, Tennessee, and Ohio. It was the only easy way to get their goods to market.

The settlers raised grain and cattle and hogs, trapped the wild animals of the forests, and shot the wild ducks and geese which covered the lakes and streams. They would load a flatboat on the Ohio, the Tennessee, or the Cumberland River and float it down to the Mississippi and on to New Orleans. At New Orleans they would transfer their load of flour and tallow and lard and their feathers and fur and hides to an ocean ship. And finally the things that they had to sell would reach the markets of Baltimore, New York, and Philadelphia.

They could not afford to carry these bulky goods to market on packhorses across the Appalachian Mountains. You see, then, how important it was for them to be able to get to the sea by way of the Mississippi.

Jefferson gets control of the Mississippi. The trouble was that the nation which owned the mouth of the Mississippi River might at any moment stop the westerners from taking their goods to the Gulf.

To prevent such a misfortune from happening to the western farmers, President Jefferson determined to buy the land along the Mississippi and around its mouth. Congress agreed to his plan, and he sent James Monroe to Paris to help Robert Livingston, our minister, to buy the land from Napoleon, the French ruler.

At first Napoleon would not listen to Livingston and Monroe, but after a while he needed money, and one day he astonished Livingston by asking what he would pay for all Louisiana. Much haggling about the price followed. Napoleon wanted to get a good price and the

Americans wanted to get Louisiana as cheaply as possible. The price was finally fixed at fifteen million dollars.

"Louisiana" meant the whole western part of the great Mississippi Valley. That land included not only the state we know today as Louisiana but eight other large states and part of four more. It spread over nearly a million square miles, an area about five times as large as France itself, from which the United States bought it.

It was a great bargain for the United States. The purchase of Louisiana made the use of the Mississippi forever safe for the western settlers. It moved the boundary of the United States westward to the Rocky Mountains. It nearly doubled the territory of the United States. The sum for which France sold this vast territory amounted to only a few cents an acre.

The United States bought Louisiana in 1803.

PRESIDENT JEFFERSON EXPLORES THE FAR WEST

Jefferson's curiosity about the West. President Jefferson had been trying to learn about the country west of the Mississippi River for more than twenty years. He wanted to know what the land was like; what animals, trees, and plants grew there; what minerals were to be found; and what opportunities there might be for trade with the Indians.

Above all, Jefferson was interested in finding a waterway across the continent to the Pacific and Asia. Like Columbus, he wanted to find a shorter route to China and the Far East. Perhaps a route across the

Signing the Louisiana Purchase Treaty, by which the United States bought about one-third of its present territory from Napoleon, emperor of France.

continent could be found, he thought, which would be quicker and cheaper than the long voyage around South America. Jefferson believed that it would be possible to discover such a route by going up one river and down another and tramping a bit across the gaps between streams.

He had it all figured out: up the James, the Potomac, or the Susquehanna; then a short tramp to the streams flowing into the Ohio or Mississippi; down those streams to the Mississippi; up the Mississippi and the Missouri to the mountains; another tramp; and, finally,

Fur trappers in the Far Northwest made friends with the Indians
and bought many skins from them.

down the Columbia River flowing into the Pacific. It
looked easy on paper, but on the ground it was very
difficult.

Several times in the past twenty years Jefferson had
believed that he was on the point of seeing the country explored, but he had always been disappointed; so
far, it had not been explored. Now he could do what
he pleased and carry out his long desire. He was President of the United States, and money and power were
in his hands. The United States owned the territory
as far as the mountains, and no other nation had a right
to stop the men that he might send to explore it.

The Lewis and Clark expedition. To lead the exploration of Louisiana and the Far West, Jefferson chose two army officers, Captain Meriwether Lewis and Captain William Clark.

Lewis was a Virginian, born near Monticello, the home of Jefferson. He was now, in 1803, twenty-nine years old. Jefferson had known him all his life, and trusted him. Clark was a few years older than Lewis, and was the brother of George Rogers Clark, who won the Northwest from the English in the War for Independence.

Under Lewis and Clark were fourteen soldiers and nine Kentucky scouts and hunters. They gathered at St. Louis in the spring of 1804, loaded their supplies into three boats, and started up the Missouri River.

They traveled slowly, making maps of the country as they went. They held councils with the Indians, made notes of the plants and animals that they saw, and wrote in their diaries at night full descriptions of all the things that they had done and seen during the day.

During the winter of 1804–1805 they camped in South Dakota. The next spring, when the snow was melted on the plain, they pressed on.

Sometimes the river ran between steep, narrow banks and was so swift that the rowers had to get out of the boats and tow them with long ropes. Sometimes there were rapids and falls that the boats could not get over at all. Then the men cut down trees, sawed round slices from the logs to use as wheels, and putting the boats on these wheels hauled them overland until they could take to the water again.

The shoes of the men wore out and they made moccasins. The sharp rocks and thorns cut through the thin deerskin moccasins and bruised and tore their feet, but there was no complaining.

Finally, after many adventures and after great hardships and suffering, they reached the very head of the Missouri River. Here it was nothing but a little brook flowing from a spring. Where they had entered the river near St. Louis it was almost a mile wide. One of the men stood with a foot on each bank of the little stream and boasted that he was big enough to straddle the great Missouri River.

Now they must cross the Rocky Mountains, find a stream on the other side, and go down it to the Pacific Ocean. Fortunately, for this part of the journey Lewis and Clark had for a guide a young Indian woman named Sacajawea (Sak-a-ja-we'a). She had been captured some years before from the Snake Indians, west of the Rocky Mountains, and was now the wife of one of Lewis's hunters.

It was necessary now to have horses, and to get them Lewis must find Indians, make friends, and buy horses from them. Captain Lewis started out with two men, and to his great delight had not gone more than five miles before he saw an Indian on horseback. He advanced slowly toward the horseman, holding out some presents to show that he was friendly; but when he got within rifle-shot the Indian wheeled and dashed away.

Next, Lewis and his two companions saw in the distance an Indian man, two squaws, and some dogs. Again Lewis tried to get close enough to talk and show

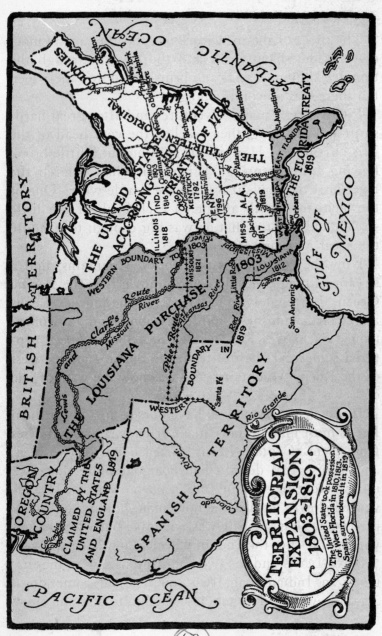

THE UNITED STATES ACCORDING TO THE TREATY OF 1783

THE ORIGINAL THIRTEEN

ATLANTIC OCEAN

Boston
New York
Philadelphia
Baltimore
O Richmond
Savannah R.
Charleston
St. Augustine

COLONIES
Hudson R.
Delaware R.
Potomac R.

BRITISH TERRITORY

THE UNITED STATES ACCORDING TO THE TREATY OF 1783

WESTERN BOUNDARY TO

OHIO 1803
Cincinnati
Ohio River
IND. 1816
Louisville
KENTUCKY 1792
Nashville
TENN. 1796
MISS. ALA.
Jackson 1817 1819
ILLINOIS 1818
MISSOURI 1821

Clark's Route
Missouri River
Lewis and
Pike's Route
Arkansas River
Little River
Red River
1819

THE LOUISIANA PURCHASE 1803

LOUISIANA 1812
New Orleans
Mobile
WEST FLORIDA EAST FLORIDA
THE FLORIDA TREATY 1819

GULF OF MEXICO

San Antonio
Santa Fé
WESTER
BOUNDARY IN 1819
Rio Grande

SPANISH TERRITORY

Colorado
River

OREGON COUNTRY
Columbia
CLAIMED BY THE UNITED STATES AND ENGLAND 1819

PACIFIC OCEAN

TERRITORIAL EXPANSION 1803-1819

The United States took possession of West Florida in 1810, 1813. Spain surrendered it in 1819.

(36)

that he was friendly, but they fled. Lewis tried to tie some presents around the necks of the dogs, but could not catch them.

After going another mile the white men found three squaws who did not run. Lewis gave them presents and

Sacajawea, an Indian girl, served as guide to Lewis and Clark when they crossed the Rocky Mountains on their trip through the Northwest wilderness to the Pacific Ocean.

proved to them that he was friendly. They then led him to their camp. Just as they arrived sixty warriors dashed up with bows and arrows drawn. But the squaws ran in front of the white men and held up their presents to show that Captain Lewis wished to be friendly.

The warriors smoked the peace pipe, and then returned with Lewis to meet Captain Clark, who was coming along with the main party. One of the chiefs turned out to be Sacajawea's brother.

Getting horses and guides from the Snake Indians, the explorers pushed on through the mountains and down to the Columbia River, where they built boats again and floated easily to the river's mouth. On November 8 they were in sight of the ocean, and Clark wrote in his diary: "Ocean in view! Oh! the joy!"

The party wintered at the mouth of the Columbia River, and in the spring started the return journey to St. Louis.

On September 23, 1806, they came again to St. Louis. With the loss of only one man, who died of sickness a few weeks after they started, they had traveled eight thousand miles. Much of this northwest wilderness had never before felt the tread of a white man's foot.

Meriwether Lewis   William Clark

By means of their explorations these men revealed to Americans the extent and resources of the western half of our country.

The importance of the Lewis and Clark expedition. The Lewis and Clark expedition opened up the geography of a vast, new region that the white people had not previously known. The explorers noticed, in particular, that the whole region swarmed with valuable fur-bearing animals, and this discovery soon drew many trappers and Indian traders into the country.

The wanderings of the fur trappers to and fro further increased the white people's knowledge of the country. The hunters discovered the easiest passes across the mountains and the easiest routes to travel from place to place. They prepared the way for the settlement of the Far Northwest as Daniel Boone had prepared the way for the settlement of Kentucky.

As a reward for Lewis's services President Jefferson appointed him governor of the Territory of Missouri. He held the office until his sudden death in 1809. Later, Clark, too, was governor of Missouri. He was appointed by President Madison and was continued in office by President Monroe.

Lieutenant Pike explores the Southwest. President Jefferson's interest in the Far Southwest was almost as keen as his interest in the Northwest. He gathered information about it for many years. He collected books and pamphlets and maps about it, and wrote to everybody who could tell him anything about the region. One of his news gatherers was Philip Nolan, a daring young man of Natchez, Mississippi, who was killed by Spaniards while hunting wild horses in Texas.

Just before Lewis and Clark got back to St. Louis in the fall of 1806, some Osage Indians came to St.

Zebulon Pike and the mountain he discovered.

Louis to see General Wilkinson. After their visit was
over they said they were afraid to go back alone to
their homes in western Kansas. General Wilkinson
therefore ordered Lieutenant Zebulon Pike to escort
them home and protect them from their enemies.

After getting the timid red men safely back to their
wigwams, Pike continued his march westward until he
was stopped in Colorado by the tall snow-capped
Rockies. He discovered Pike's Peak, which was named
for him, and then turned southward to explore the country toward Santa Fé.

Both Colorado and New Mexico then belonged to
Spain, and the Spanish government feared and dis-

trusted foreigners. Pike was arrested near Santa Fé and started to Mexico City under guard.

Though Pike told the Spaniards that he was a friendly explorer, they would not at first believe him. Later, however, they changed their minds, set him free, and allowed him to return to St. Louis through Texas and Arkansas.

Pike's diaries were soon published, and we may be sure that Thomas Jefferson read them eagerly. They told about the geography of the Southwest, just as the reports of Lewis and Clark had told of the Northwest.

Pike's visit to Santa Fé led later to an important trading business between the merchants of St. Louis and the merchants of Santa Fé. At first long trains of pack horses carried the goods, but when their hoofs had beaten out the Santa Fé Trail, covered wagons took their place.

THE UNITED STATES GETS FLORIDA

Spain gives up Florida. In 1819 President James Monroe finished the job that he had begun when he bought Louisiana for President Jefferson in 1803. He got Florida from Spain. The United States now owned all the vast territory south of the Canada boundary, from the Atlantic Ocean as far west as the Rocky Mountains.

Thomas Jefferson had the pleasure of knowing before his death on the Fourth of July, 1826, that the western boundary would in all probability soon extend to the Pacific Ocean. We shall learn in later chapters of this book how Jefferson's dream came true, how the

United States spread the rest of the way from ocean to ocean.

A SHORT STORY TO TELL

As long as a foreign country owned the mouth of the Mississippi River it might keep the American settlers in Kentucky and Tennessee and Ohio from sending their goods down the river to market. In order to get possession of the Mississippi River, President Jefferson bought Louisiana from France in 1803.

President Jefferson wanted very much to find an easy way across the continent to the Pacific Ocean, and so he sent Lewis and Clark to explore Louisiana and the country beyond the Rocky Mountains. They went up the Missouri River to its head and then crossed the mountains and went down the Columbia River to its mouth. When they returned, they told of the many wild animals that they had seen during their journey, and fur trappers and Indian traders soon began to go into the Far West. They blazed the way to the Pacific Ocean in the same way that Boone and the earlier pioneers had blazed the way to the Mississippi. While Lewis and Clark were exploring the Far Northwest, Lieutenant Pike was exploring the Southwest, which still belonged to Spain.

In 1819 President Monroe obtained Florida for the United States.

LEARNING FROM A MAP

1. Show on a map the route by which farmers in Ohio and Kentucky would send their goods to market. Explain why this was the best way.

2. Show on a map the way that Jefferson thought people might be able to travel from coast to coast by water.

3. Show the land which the United States got from France and from Spain.

4. Trace the route taken by Lewis and Clark.

5. Point out and name the states that were made out of the Louisiana Purchase.

THOSE WHO HELPED

6. Tell what each of the people listed below did to help the United States spread its control beyond the Mississippi River.

James Monroe	Meriwether Lewis
Robert Livingston	William Clark
Thomas Jefferson	Zebulon Pike
Napoleon	Sacajawea

WORDS TO EXPLAIN

7. Tell what the underlined words mean in the following sentences:

France and the United States, after haggling over the price of Louisiana, agreed on fifteen million dollars.

This was a bargain for the territory cost but a few cents an acre.

Lewis and Clark had to tow their boats when the Missouri River became too swift.

The men with Lewis and Clark had to make moccasins before their journey ended.

These explorers blazed the way to the Pacific Ocean.

THE WAR OF 1812
SHOWING STATES ADMITTED TO 1812

pront 34 r 55

UNIT TWO

THE NATION LEARNS TO STAND ALONE

The United States gained its independence in a war with England. For several years after the war, it was a very weak nation. Many of our own leaders feared that it would break up and divide into thirteen separate states.

Foreign nations took advantage of its weakness and treated it very much as they pleased. England would not let our ships enter its ports to unload goods or take on cargoes. It wanted English ships to have all the profit of carrying goods from England to the United States and from the United States to England. English warships searched American vessels to see if they had any English sailors on board. If they found any, they took them off and made them work on English ships. France also mistreated the United States, and sometimes seized American vessels that went into French ports.

All this mistreatment by foreign nations came to an end after the second war with England, in 1812. The United States proved in that war that it could take care of itself. At the same time the people of the United States began to feel pride in the greatness of their nation. They felt that it was no longer weak. It was able to stand alone.

Factories sprang up. Americans began to make at home goods that they had formerly bought from Europe. In the old days they had raised cotton and wool in America. They shipped the wool to England and France, and then bought it back in the form of cloth. Now, however, they began to make their own cloth, their own tools, their own machinery, and nearly

(45)

everything else that they needed for their comfort and happiness.

More and more people began to take part in the government. As long as the country that we now call the United States belonged to England, very few people had the right to vote and hold office. But the Americans believed in "government by the people." Andrew Jackson was called "the people's President." His motto was: "Let the people rule." He meant by this motto that all free men should have the right to vote and hold office.

The inventiveness of the Americans has added greatly to the comfort and happiness of the people and to the wealth and power of our nation. Let us see what we have gained from the cotton gin, the steamboat, the railroad, the sewing machine, the telegraph, and the mechanical reaper.

BOOKS TO READ FOR UNIT TWO

Stone, G. L., and Fickett, M. G., *Days and Deeds a Hundred Years Ago* (D. C. Heath and Company).

Hayes, Marjorie, *Little House On Wheels* (Harcourt, Brace and Company).

Swift, H. H., *Little Black Nose; the Story of a Pioneer* (Harcourt, Brace and Company).

Nathan, Mrs. A. G., *Farmer Sows His Wheat* (G. P. Putnam and Sons).

Perry, F. M., *Four American Inventors* (American Book Company).

Barstow, C. L., *A New Nation* (D. Appleton-Century Company).

Van Metre, T. W., *Trains, Tracks and Travel* (Simmons-Boardman Company).

Chapter V

THE SECOND WAR WITH ENGLAND

John C. Calhoun

ENGLAND MISTREATS THE UNITED STATES

England searches American ships. About the time that Jefferson became President of the United States, England got into a war with France. Then England, in order to injure France, tried to stop everybody from trading with France. In order to keep American ships from carrying food and war supplies to France, commanders of English warships made a practice of stopping vessels flying the Stars and Stripes, and searching them. If the English commanders found a ship on the way to France, they took it to England.

James Madison was Jefferson's Secretary of State. Many times he and Jefferson sent word to the English government, warning it to leave American ships alone.

They said that English warships had no right to search vessels flying the American flag. But England kept on stopping vessels and paid no attention to Jefferson and Madison.

England takes sailors from American ships. Another troublesome thing that England did was to have the commanders of its warships stop American vessels to see if they had any Englishmen among the crews. England needed sailors for its vessels. If the officers found any English sailors on American ships, they took them off and put them to work on English ships.

Madison and Jefferson protested against this practice. They said that the waters of the ocean were like a public road and that the ships of all nations had the right to sail the open sea without being stopped.

To make matters worse, the English officers sometimes took American sailors and made them work on English ships. The trouble was that sometimes they could not tell whether a sailor was an American or an Englishman.

The worst case of this sort happened toward the end of President Jefferson's second term in the White House. In this case the English man-of-war *Leopard* stopped the American warship *Chesapeake*.

Commodore James Barron, commanding the *Chesapeake,* stopped when the English vessel signaled him, because he understood that the commander of the *Leopard* wanted to give him some mail. Instead, however, a young English officer came on board and demanded four sailors who, he said, had deserted from the English navy.

The Chesapeake, Captain Lawrence, captured by the Shannon.

When Commodore Barron would not give them up, the *Leopard* fired a broadside and disabled the *Chesapeake* before Barron could get ready to fire a shot. Then the English officer returned and got the four men, while the badly damaged *Chesapeake* limped back into harbor for repairs.

Jefferson and Madison try to avoid war. Nearly every-where the American people now insisted on going to war against England. It was bad enough, they said, for England to search vessels that were carrying freight across the ocean under the American flag. It had no right to do that; but its attack on a warship of the United States was the same as an attack on our President himself. It was an insult that nothing but war could wipe out.

President Jefferson, however, still believed that

without going to war he could make England stop mis-
treating the United States. Jefferson went out of office
in 1809, and Madison became President. The quarrel
with England still went on, but the tide was about to
turn.

The "War Hawks" declare war. In December, 1811,
a remarkable group of young men went to Congress
for the first time. John C. Calhoun of South Carolina
and Henry Clay of Kentucky were among the leaders
of these young members of Congress. Daniel Webster,
of New England, came in the next session, and for
nearly forty years these three great men shared all the
honors that Congress could give them.

This group of young congressmen were proud of
their country, they were proud of its strength and they
wanted war. The old members of Congress called them
"War Hawks," and still tried to keep out of war. But
the War Hawks kept shouting, "War, war;" and on
June 18, 1812, Congress voted for war.

If the War Hawks had waited a few weeks longer,
the war could have been avoided, for England had
already agreed to quit stopping ships and taking
sailors. But it took six weeks for news to cross the Atlantic in those days and the War Hawks did not know
that they had won their point before the war began.

THE WAR OF 1812

The brilliant work of the navy. The wonderful fighting of the little American navy was a great surprise.
The United States had only sixteen warships when
the war began. They could do nothing in battle, of

course, against England's giant fleet; but they put out to sea at the beginning of the war, and sailed around, each one alone, looking for enemy ships.

Each ship had to take care of itself. When the commanders sighted an enemy that they dared not meet, they ran; but ships of their own size they fought.

The most famous American vessel was the *Constitution*. The people called it *"Old Ironsides."* In August, 1812, it wrecked the British ship *Guerriere* after a battle of only thirty minutes. In December, 1812, it captured the *Java.* And throughout the war it won every battle that it fought.

The unfortunate *Chesapeake* was captured, after a duel in which Captain James Lawrence, its heroic commander, was mortally wounded. Lawrence died, murmuring, "Don't give up the ship!"

But the odds were too great on the ocean. The English ships were too strong for the weaker American navy, and there were too many of them. Before the end of the war, all but one or two of the gallant American vessels were captured or "bottled up."

On Lake Erie and Lake Champlain, however, the little American fleets won great victories, and kept the British from sending armies from Canada.

In September, 1813, Captain Oliver Hazard Perry captured the entire British fleet of six vessels in Lake Erie. He reported his victory in one sentence: "We have met the enemy and they are ours." Perry was then only twenty-eight years old.

The hero of Lake Champlain was Captain Thomas MacDonough. In 1814 he defeated the British fleet of

sixteen vessels at Plattsburg, New York. By this
victory he saved New York from invasion. Captain
MacDonough was a young man only thirty years old.

The failure of the war on land. Neither the Americans
nor the English did good fighting on land. Three times
our armies tried to go into Canada. Each time they
failed. The English were equally unsuccessful in
their efforts to break into the United States from
Canada.

In August, 1814, the English used their powerful
navy to land an army on Chesapeake Bay. The army
marched against Washington. President and Mrs.
Madison hastily fled. Congress had already fled. The
British marched into the city without firing a shot.
They set fire to the White House, the Capitol, and
other public buildings, destroyed many valuable
papers, and then left.

The English then tried to take Baltimore. Their
commander vowed that he would winter in Baltimore,
even if it "rained militia," but he failed. His ships
could not get close enough to the city to batter it down
with their guns. He kept up a bombardment all one
night, and then gave it up.

It was during the bombardment of Baltimore by the
English fleet, that Francis Scott Key, an American
prisoner of war on one of the English ships, wrote *The
Star Spangled Banner.*

Andrew Jackson wins the Battle of New Orleans. The
last battle of the war on land was fought near New
Orleans, January 8, 1815. This battle gave General
Andrew Jackson the name of being a great soldier.

Peace had been signed by the English and American representatives in Europe two weeks before the Battle of New Orleans, but the news had not reached America.

General Andrew Jackson's victory at New Orleans. The Battle of New Orleans would never have been fought if there had been cable or radio to carry the news that peace had already been signed.

In the Battle of New Orleans Jackson, with five thousand men, defeated eight thousand of the best soldiers in the English army. His Kentucky and Tennessee riflemen mowed down the charging English by hundreds. The English lost all of their generals, seven hundred men killed, fourteen hundred wounded, and five hundred prisoners. Jackson lost eight killed and thirteen wounded. For his success in the Battle of New Orleans, and because of his rapid marches and tough endurance in Indian campaigns, Jackson was called "Old Hickory."

The Battle of New Orleans had no effect on the war, of course, because peace had already been signed and the war was over, but it gave the Americans a feeling of great pride. They had crushed a strong English army, the best that England could send against them. They knew that their country need never again fear to fight when its cause was just.

The peace treaty. The peace was signed on Christmas eve, December 24, 1814. This treaty marked the end of the second war of the United States with England. It is to be hoped that there will never be another.

A SHORT STORY TO TELL

In 1803, the same year that President Jefferson bought Louisiana, England got into a war with France. During the war English warships captured many American vessels which were carrying food and war goods to France. They also stopped American ships on the ocean and took sailors from them to sail their own ships. Both President Jefferson and President Madison tried to get England to let our ships alone, but it kept right on taking ships and sailors.

Finally, in 1812, Congress declared war against England. The war lasted two years and a half. The American armies tried to take Canada and failed. The English armies tried to invade the United States and failed. The most famous battle of the war was the

Battle of New Orleans. In this battle General Andrew Jackson, of Tennessee, with about five thousand men, defeated an English army of eight thousand men.

Commodore Perry fought the most famous naval battle of the war on Lake Erie. In this battle he captured the whole English fleet.

STORY SUGGESTIONS

1. These combinations of words appear in the story of the second war with England. What part of the story does each combination of words bring to your mind?

mortally wounded   kept up a bombardment
"Old Hickory"   "War Hawks"
"Don't Give Up the Ship"   "Old Ironsides"
      "We have met the enemy and they are ours."

WHAT DO YOU THINK?

2. Would the radio have helped to prevent the Battle of New Orleans or have made it unnecessary to fight the War of 1812? Explain your answer.

3. Could the second war with England be called a second War for Independence? Explain your answer.

STORIES TO READ

4. Read the stories about "The Second War With England," in *A New Nation* by C. L. Barstow (D. Appleton-Century Company) pp. 43–71 or in *Makers and Defenders of America* by A. E. Foote and A. W. Skinner (American Book Company) pages 141–152.

Chapter VI

OUR NATION GROWS STRONG

James Monroe

AMERICANS LEARN TO USE MACHINES

The beginning of American factories. The War of 1812 taught the people of the United States to live on what they could make for themselves—to get on without buying from Europe. Before the war most of our people made their living by some sort of farming. They raised crops and shipped what they did not use to Europe. In Europe they exchanged their farm stuff for factory-made goods. They bought fine cotton, linen, and woolen cloth; fine gloves, furniture, and tools.

Of course there was always a good deal of spinning, weaving, and shoemaking in the colonies. Men made some furniture and tools at home. But the people bought most of their fine things in Europe.

Picking cotton on a southern plantation.

The war put a stop to our trading with Europe. We could no longer send our crops to Europe nor bring fine manufactured goods from Europe. What was to be done?

There is a saying that "Necessity is the mother of invention." The saying means that people who cannot get what they want in any other way must find a way to make it, and that is what the Americans now did. They built factories and began to make for themselves the things that they had been buying in Europe.

At first the American factories gave most of their time to making three things: cotton cloth, woolen cloth, and things made of iron. The iron things included tools, machinery, pots, kettles, and other household articles.

England tries to ruin the American factories. After the war was over, the American factories had a hard time because English merchants and factory owners tried to put them out of business. Englishmen wanted to keep on selling their own goods to the Americans, and they fought the American factories in two ways.

First, they refused to sell the Americans any factory machinery. England was the greatest clothmaking country in the world. Its machinery was the best and its factory hands were the most skillful. The Americans would have been glad to buy machines in England; but as the English refused to sell machines, the Americans kept on making their own machines. And they learned to make them better and better until they became as good as the English machines. Soon factory hands in the United States became as skillful as the English workmen.

The second way in which the English merchants and factory-owners fought the American factories was to ship great quantities of goods to America and sell them below cost. This scheme almost ruined the young American factories, for people like a bargain. Americans bought the cheap English goods, and in that way helped England fight the American factories. Of course, the American factories would have to close their doors and go out of business if they could not sell their goods.

To save the American factories from being put out

of business, Congress passed a law putting a heavy tax on goods brought into the United States from foreign countries. The tax raised the price of the English goods so high that people went back to buying the goods of the American factories.

Soon many millions of dollars were being invested in American factories and hundreds of thousands of men, women, and children were making their living by running the factory machines.

Other thousands of men were engaged at the same time, of course, in raising the cotton and wool and mining the iron and making the machines with which the factories worked.

Thus the War of 1812 was in some ways a good thing for the United States. It made the Americans learn to depend upon themselves for all the things they needed to live on. They had always been able to raise all the farm stuff that they needed. Now they were able also to do their own manufacturing.

The cotton gin. The factories for making cotton cloth could never have been started, if a machine called a cotton gin had not been invented.

Very little cotton was raised in the United States until after the gin was invented. It was so slow and costly to get the seed out of the cotton by hand that farmers could not make money by raising cotton. It is said that a man working all day could pull but a pound or two of cotton off of the seed.

In 1793, Eli Whitney, a young Massachusetts school teacher, was spending the winter teaching the children on a plantation near Savannah, Georgia. Talking one

An early cotton mill. After the invention of the cotton gin, more
and more mills were built, and more and more cotton was raised.

day about cotton raising, somebody said what a fine
thing it would be if there were a machine which would
get the seed out of the cotton. Such a machine would
save much time and labor, and would make cotton raising a paying business.

The idea of making such a machine took hold of
young Whitney's mind. His father had a machine shop
in Massachusetts, and Eli had worked in the shop
when he was a boy. He was handy with tools. So he
set to work and within a few weeks he had made a
machine that ginned fifty pounds of cotton a day.

This machine solved the problem. Whitney and other inventors made improvements which soon made it possible for one machine to gin a thousand pounds a day. Cotton raising immediately jumped to a leading place in southern farming. Many planters began to raise almost nothing to sell but cotton.

Two years before Whitney invented the gin, the South shipped only thirty-four hundred bales of cotton to Europe. Ten years after the gin began to be used, sixty-seven thousand bales were sent to Europe. These figures show how fast the raising of cotton increased after the invention of the gin. All the cotton was raised in the South because cotton will not grow in a cold country.

After the War of 1812 the southern planters shipped much of their cotton to the northern factories instead of to Europe.

The important effect of the factories. It was good for the people of the United States to be able to make what they needed and to live independently of the rest of the world. From now on Americans could not only raise the farm crops that they needed. They could also make their own clothing, their own tools and machinery, and their own war materials in case of war. They had within their own territory all the things that the people needed to live comfortably in peace or to fight successfully in war. Few nations are so fortunate.

THE UNITED STATES WARNS EUROPE

James Monroe. James Monroe was the fifth President of the United States. The four Presidents who had served before him were Washington, John Adams, Jefferson, and Madison. Adams was from Massachusetts. The others were from Virginia, and Monroe was from Virginia, too.

Monroe was born April 28, 1758. When the War for Independence began he was a student at William and Mary College. He left college to join the army. He was with Washington at the battle of Trenton and attracted attention there by his bravery. He was wounded at Trenton, and left the army for a time; but returned when he recovered from his wound, and fought bravely in many battles.

After the war he served in the Continental Congress, was twice Governor of Virginia, and was sent to both France and England to represent the United States as minister. For four years he was in the United States Senate, and while Madison was President he was Secretary of State and then Secretary of War. He knew all the work of the government.

Monroe was so successful in pleasing all parts of the country during his first term in the Presidency (1817–1821), that he was reëlected with only one vote against him. His second term was even more successful than his first, and was called the "era of good feeling."

President Monroe's most famous act was a message he sent Congress, in December, 1823, warning European governments not to interfere in American affairs. This warning is called the Monroe Doctrine.

The story of the Monroe Doctrine. The reason for President Monroe's message was this: Mexico and South America had just gained their independence from the king of Spain. Several of the other kings in Europe were planning to help the king of Spain get them back into his power so that he could rule them. When President Monroe heard what these kings were planning, he wrote the Monroe Doctrine.

The Monroe Doctrine warned European rulers that they must not take any more land in America and that they must not disturb the governments of Mexico and South America and Central America. It said that they must let the people of those countries govern themselves in any way they pleased.

The United States grows up. By the end of President Monroe's second term we may say that the United States was a grown-up nation. It could raise its own food. It could manufacture its own goods. It could hold America for the Americans and for the people of other countries who wished to become Americans.

A SHORT STORY TO TELL

Even after Washington and his brave soldiers won the independence of the United States in the first war with England, our country was weak, like a little child that can hardly stand alone. Most of the American people were farmers. There were no great factories in the country as there are today. Merchants shipped farm goods across the ocean and brought back from Europe, cloth, hats and gloves, furniture, tools, and a great many other things made in Europe.

While the second war with England was going on, the Americans began to build factories and make their own factory goods. Our country was growing up. It was learning to stand alone. The people were learning to depend upon themselves. They were learning to raise on the farms and make in the factories everything that they had to use.

For a long time the most important factories were those that made cotton and woolen cloth. But it was the invention of the cotton gin by Eli Whitney in 1793 that made the cotton factories multiply and grow.

While Monroe was President he wrote a message telling the European governments to let all the American countries alone. His warning meant: "America for the Americans."

PROGRESS IN AMERICA

1. Give examples to show that the United States was growing into a strong nation.

2. Give examples of the products made in early American factories.

3. Give examples of the things that made it possible for American factories to increase their business.

4. Give examples of the way England tried to hinder our progress in manufacturing.

LET'S PRETEND

5. Pretend you are New England mill owners just after the War of 1812. You are having a meeting to discuss why it is so hard to make a success of your business, and what can be done to improve business.

6. Pretend you are a group of southern farmers who are discussing the effects of the invention of the cotton gin.

Chapter VII

THE RULE OF ANDREW JACKSON

Andrew Jackson

FROM A LOG CABIN TO THE WHITE HOUSE

The son of an Irish farmer. Andrew Jackson was the seventh President of the United States. Those who had held the office of president before him were George Washington, John Adams, Thomas Jefferson, James Madison, James Monroe, and John Quincy Adams. All of these were men of wealth and high social position. They had grown up in comfortable homes, and all of them except Washington were college-trained men. Jackson had had a very different sort of childhood and youth. His parents were poor and he had little time to go to school.

Andrew Jackson was the son of Irish parents who came to America just two years before he was born.

(65)

They settled in the western hills, almost on the line between North Carolina and South Carolina. There, after his father's death, Andrew grew up in the home of an aunt with whom his mother went to live.

We have already seen Jackson winning the battle of New Orleans. He fought his first battle in the War for Independence before he was fourteen. A few months after this first battle, he and his brother Robert were captured by a band of English cavalry soldiers. The commander ordered Andrew to shine his boots. The boy replied that he was a soldier and a prisoner of war, and refused. The cruel officer struck him over the head with his sword. Jackson carried to his grave a scar from the blow.

When Jackson was nineteen he moved westward to Tennessee. He settled at Nashville and began to practice law. He was successful and popular. The people liked him and elected him to many offices, but he was above all other things a soldier, and liked to lead soldiers. He became a general during the War of 1812.

Jackson a marked man. After the battle of New Orleans General Jackson was the military hero of the country. Everybody admired him and talked about him; and he gave them a good deal to talk about.

During an Indian war in 1818 he chased a band of Creek and Seminole Indians into Florida, which then belonged to Spain. He captured a Spanish fort in Florida, burned Indian villages, and hanged two Englishmen whom he found among the Indians, because he believed they had been helping the Indians to make raids into Georgia and Alabama.

Spain demanded that he be punished and dismissed from the army for going into Spanish territory. England complained about the death of the two Englishmen. The country hummed with excitement. The papers were filled with talk of war.

But our government would not punish Jackson and it would not dismiss him from the army. Finally England was satisfied with apologies and explanations, and Spain sold Florida to the United States. Then President Monroe appointed Jackson governor of Florida. In 1823 Tennessee sent him to the United States Senate, and the next year made him a candidate for the presidency.

Jackson elected President in 1828. Andrew Jackson first became a candidate for the presidency in the election of 1824, but failed. The election was won by John Quincy Adams of Massachusetts.

Adams had already held many high offices in the government, and was an able president. But Jackson disliked Adams and immediately decided to run for the presidency again in the next election.

The people of the West wanted Andrew Jackson. They said they were tired of Presidents from the old states. They wanted "a man of the people," a man from the West who would give the people their rights. "Old Hickory" was the man for them—and he was! When the votes were counted, Andrew Jackson had most of the votes and was elected President. Two years later John Quincy Adams was elected to Congress from Massachusetts, and served in that office for seventeen years. He died at Washington in 1848.

The people went wild with joy, and flocked to Washington by thousands to see their hero go into office. They crowded the streets of the capital in their coonskin caps and ill-fitting homespun clothes. They swarmed through the White House, shouting loud greetings and wiping their muddy boots on the costly carpets.

Fashionable people in Washington looked on with surprise, and shrugged their shoulders in amusement. With a backwoods Indian fighter in the presidency, there would be no more fine parties at the White House, they said, and Washington society would be very dull indeed.

Sober business men and shipowners, bankers, and manufacturers shook their heads in doubt. They knew that although Jackson was entirely honest, he knew little about business. They feared that in his efforts to help all the people he might do things that would upset business conditions and bring on lean, hard times.

But, although Jackson was the friend of the farmers, the factory hands, and other working people, he knew that the interests of the business men must also be looked after. He considered himself the President of all the United States, not the President of one class of people or of a single section of the country. He believed that the laws should be enforced everywhere.

GOVERNMENT FOR THE PEOPLE

Jackson's motto, "Let the people rule." Jackson believed in a government "for the people, by the people." He meant by these words a government that would

Indians got petroleum from oil-covered pools by dipping a blanket and wringing it into a bowl. They used petroleum as medicine long before white men found so many uses for it and drilled oil wells.

always work to help the people, and in which people of all classes should share the offices. He believed, too, that nobody should hold a public office for a long time, but that the government jobs should change often in order to give more men a chance to hold them. His favorite motto was, "Let the people rule."

Jackson saves the public lands for the people. In carrying on "government for the people" Jackson decided that the land that the government owned ought to be sold only to settlers who wanted homes and farms for their families.

It had been the government's practice to sell its land to anyone who offered the most money for it. Jackson found that some rich men were getting much of the choicest government land, because they could offer to pay more for it than home seekers could afford to pay. Jackson stopped this practice and kept the land in the hands of the government to be sold for homesteads.

Jackson moves the Indians to the Indian Territory. Jackson helped the home-seeking settlers in another way. He moved the Indians from the states east of the Mississippi River to the Indian Territory, now the State of Oklahoma.

The Cherokee, Choctaw, Creek, and Chickasaw Indians claimed many million acres of land in the four states of Georgia, Alabama, Mississippi, and Tennessee. By moving the Indians Jackson freed these lands for white settlers. Years later, coal and oil were discovered in the Indian Territory, and some of the grandchildren of the Indians that Jackson moved became very wealthy.

The end of Jackson's presidency. The people liked Jackson's idea of "government for the people, by the people," and showed that they did by keeping him in the presidency for two terms. When he left the White House and returned to his Tennessee plantation, men from all parts of the country paid him honor.

He continued for eight more years to be a leader in politics. Men visited him at his home, the Hermitage, to get his views on public questions. Candidates running for office always tried to get him to help them, for they knew that Jackson's backing would get votes.

Jackson died in 1845, and most of the great men with whom he played his part on the stage of American history soon followed him to the grave. His old enemy, John Quincy Adams, died in 1848; Calhoun died in 1850; and Henry Clay and Daniel Webster died in 1852. New problems were facing the country, and new leaders must solve them.

The men of Jackson's time did not always agree with one another and work together, but each did what he thought was right, and they wore themselves out in the service of their country. We should be grateful to them and honor them.

JACKSON'S SUCCESSORS IN THE PRESIDENCY

Eight Presidents who followed Jackson. We cannot tell the whole history of our country in this little book. We can tell only the most interesting and most important parts of it. For the next twenty-four years after Jackson went out of office the Presidents were good men, but we need not read about them here. You can learn who they were from this list:

Name	In Office	Elected from
Martin Van Buren	1837–1841	New York
William H. Harrison	March 4, 1841– April 4, 1841	Ohio
John Tyler	April 4, 1841–1845	Virginia
James K. Polk	1845–1849	Tennessee
Zachary Taylor	1849–July 9, 1850	Louisiana
Millard Fillmore	July 9, 1850–1853	New York
Franklin Pierce	1853–1857	New Hampshire
James Buchanan	1857–1861	Pennsylvania

Pioneer people were usually friendly. Those who traveled often stopped to see acquaintances and exchange news.

A SHORT STORY TO TELL

Andrew Jackson was the son of a poor Irish farmer. He became a famous man when he won the Battle of New Orleans against an English army nearly twice as large as his own. Everywhere, in all parts of the United States, the people admired and talked about him, but he was especially popular in the West. The people called him "Old Hickory."

When Jackson became President in 1828, he tried to run the government for the benefit of the people. His motto was: "Let the People Rule." He gave government offices to many people who had never held office before. He stopped the sale of government land to rich business men because he wanted to save it for poor people who needed it for farms. He got Congress to set aside the Indian Territory in what is now the state of Oklahoma as a home for the Indians. Then he moved large tribes of Indians into the territory so that white settlers could move into the Indian lands in the old states. He sometimes used bad judgment and did things that he ought not to have done, but he tried always to help the people, and they were grateful to him.

MAP STUDY

1. Find on a map the part of the United States that was the Indian Territory into which Jackson moved the Indians.

2. Find the states from which the Indians were moved and name the four tribes of Indians who left these states.

DO YOU KNOW

3. What did the people of the West mean when they said they wanted "a man of the people" for president?

4. What did Jackson mean by "Let the People Rule"?

STORY TELLING

5. Choose one of these stories to tell to the class. The books listed on page 46 will help you.

Andrew Jackson as a boy.

Andrew Jackson as an Indian fighter.

Andrew Jackson at New Orleans.

Andrew Jackson takes office as President.

Andrew Jackson as President.

Chapter VIII

INVENTIONS AND DISCOVERIES CHANGE AMERICAN LIFE

Robert Fulton

OLD WAYS OF TRAVEL

The horse, the canoe, and the sailboat. Of all the changes that have taken place since the days of our colonial forefathers, none are more important than the changes in the way we travel, ship goods from place to place, and send and receive messages.

Our ancestors had to make whatever they wanted or wait so long to get it that often when they got it they no longer wanted it. Today the steamboat, the railroad, and the telegraph make it easy for us to get what we want when we want it.

The first settlers in our country did not travel much. On Sundays they rode horseback to church, sometimes

eight or ten miles away, and on court days the men
gathered at the courthouse; but for the most part they
stayed at home. There was so much work to be done
in the new country, and so few hands to do it.

For a long time the roads were mere trails, fit only
for horseback riding. Hotels, or taverns and inns as
they were called, were few and bad. The food they
served was poorly cooked, and the beds, besides being
dirty, must often be shared with a stranger or even two.

Because of the bad roads and poor hotels women
almost never traveled, and men did not make long
journeys if they could help it. When they had to go
somewhere, they went as much of the way as possible
by water. Farms and plantations fronting on rivers
and bays had canoes, rowboats, and small sailboats.
In these the traveler went to the nearest seaport and
there took an ocean-going ship for the rest of his trip.

When the United States became independent, it was
necessary for the different parts of the country to have
more to do with one another than they had to have
as mere colonies of England. The national capital,
where the government was carried on, was first at
New York, then at Philadelphia, and finally at Washington. Because of this fact it was necessary to improve
the roads from the north and the south to the capital,
so that traveling would be easier.

For a while the stagecoach seemed the last word
in rapid and comfortable travel. Drawn by four or six
horses, which were changed at frequent "stages" or
stations, the lumbering coaches made an average speed
of four or five miles an hour. Horse flesh could do no

A trial trip of the Clermont

more; some other way of travel must be invented if greater speed was wanted.

THE COMING OF THE STEAMBOAT

Robert Fulton runs boats by steam. In England the steam engine had already been invented, and was being used to run machinery in factories. If it could be used to move wagons and carriages, the problem of rapid travel and cheap and rapid carrying of freight would be settled.

In 1807, near the end of Jefferson's second term, Robert Fulton succeeded in running the first successful steamboat, the *Clermont,* up the Hudson River from New York to Albany at a speed of five miles an hour.

The story of Fulton's steamboat.* Fulton was born in Pennsylvania, near Philadelphia. He was ten years old when the American Revolution began, and grew to young manhood during the war. He showed great skill in drawing pictures, and, as photography had not then been invented, he made much money painting small portraits of people who wanted their "pictures taken."

He was always interested in machinery, and during a trip to England he made a study of the steam engine. The idea of making a steamboat took hold of him. He could think of nothing else. How could he make steam work paddles and drive a boat through the water? He asked himself the question over and over again. He was sure it could be done, but at first he did not see quite how. And he needed money to make experiments. Where could he get the money?

In Paris he talked over his ideas with Robert Livingston, the minister of the United States who, with James Monroe, bought Louisiana. You remember that Livingston was a member of Jefferson's committee which wrote the Declaration of Independence. He belonged to a wealthy New York family, and was already eager to see steamboats on the Hudson River. He agreed to furnish the money necessary for making the experiment, and Fulton went to work in earnest.

If he could build a boat with a big paddle wheel on each side, and connect an engine with the wheels so as to make them turn round and round in the water, the boat would go. After several unsuccessful attempts he

---

*The honor of inventing the steamboat belongs to John Fitch of Kentucky.

brought over from England one of the newest and best engines and set it up in the *Clermont.* And it worked!

As the first steamboat puffed its way upstream, clouds of smoke pouring from the smokestack and sparks showering the deck, wild animals fled in terror from the banks of the river, and the frightened settlers along the way believed that the world was coming to an end. They had never dreamed of such a terrifying monster. But the terror soon passed, and the steamboat remained.

In a few more years boats were being built on all the rivers. In 1811 the *New Orleans* was finished at Pittsburgh, ready for its first trip down the Ohio and the Mississippi to New Orleans. In 1817 the first boat steamed up the Mississippi on a complete voyage from New Orleans to St. Louis. The great river had found its master. The steamboat had come.

ROADS AND CANALS

The merchants want roads. As more and more people moved into the back country and across the mountains, the cities near the Atlantic coast saw the need of building good roads and canals. They wanted to be able to sell their goods to the settlers and bring back cheaply the grain, meat and skins that the settlers had to sell.

Baltimore gets the Chesapeake and Ohio Canal. Baltimore built a good road to the Potomac River near Washington. Above that point the river is blocked by huge boulders and rapids and falls, so that boats cannot use it above Washington. But a ditch or canal was dug along the bank of the river and filled with water from the stream; then boats could be towed up and down the canal, loaded with all sorts of goods.

When the canal could be built no higher into the foothills of the Appalachians, the road began again and crossed the mountains to Wheeling and Pittsburgh on the Ohio River. This was the route of the Chesapeake and Ohio Canal and the Cumberland Road.

A canal boat was long and narrow. It could be loaded with many wagon-loads of goods, and then a single horse, ridden by a boy, could walk along the bank and tow it. James A. Garfield, who became President of the United States in 1881, was once a towpath boy on a canal in Ohio.

The Philadelphia merchants had a way to the West up the Susquehanna River and the Juniata River to Pittsburgh. There the Philadelphia route connected with the Ohio.

The Erie Canal. The greatest of the canals was the Erie Canal, which connected New York City with Lake Erie. This route from New York to the West followed the Hudson River up to Albany, where the canal began. Following the course of the Mohawk River from that point, the great "ditch" finally reached Lake Erie, three hundred and fifty miles away.

The Erie Canal was completed in 1825, the year that John Quincy Adams became President. It was due almost wholly to the work of Governor De Witt Clinton of New York. Before it was finished some people spoke of it with a sneer, calling it "Clinton's Folly." They said that the Erie Canal would never repay the state and the men who furnished the money to dig it.

Canal boats were towed by horses that walked along a tow-path on the bank. People traveled by canal boat before there were railroads, but canals long ago went out of use except for freight.

But, as often happens, those who laughed quickly found themselves mistaken. In the first two years after the canal was opened a million and a half dollars was collected in tolls, or charges, from people who used the canal. The total cost of digging the canal was repaid in four or five years. After that the collections continued to increase and were mostly a clear profit. The people who had talked about "Clinton's Folly" had nothing more to say.

Both the Chesapeake and Ohio Canal and the Erie

Canal are still in use, but they are used now only for slow freight. Railroads run along the banks of each and carry most of the freight that used to go by boat.

Roads and canals make the Union stronger. Improved roads and canals increased the speed and comfort of travel. They brought the different sections of the country close together by making it cheap and easy to ship goods and carry mail. In this way the roads and canals helped to make the United States strong, helped to make it a nation of united people.

THE BEGINNING OF RAILROADS

Horse-car railroads. The next step forward in cheap and rapid travel and carrying freight came with the railroad, and the invention of the steam engine to draw trains over the roads.

The "iron horse" carried people at a speed of about twenty miles an hour. Compared with travel by canal boat, stagecoach, or horse-back this was breathless speed.

The first railroads were exactly what the word says; they were roads made of rails. Rails, or pieces of timber about four inches square, were placed end to end and nailed to cross-pieces, called "ties."

Wagons for carrying freight and coaches for carrying passengers were drawn over these rails by horses, just as horses towed boats on the canals. Wheels with flanges, or specially made rims, held the cars to the track. When traffic became heavy, flat strips of iron were nailed on the rails, to keep them from wearing out. The next step was to use all-iron rails instead of the wooden rails. In our day rails are made of steel.

George Stephenson makes the first railroad engine. The problem now was to make a steam engine to pull the cars on the railroad. Fulton had made steam run his boat. Who could harness steam to the railroad? Many inventors spent all their waking hours thinking how to do this, and some may have dreamed about it at night.

George Stephenson, an Englishman, was the first to solve the problem. In 1829, the year that Jackson became President of the United States, Stephenson ran an engine on a road in England twenty-nine miles an hour. Because it went so fast, he named it the *Rocket*.

The first railroad engines in the United States. The next year after Stephenson built the *Rocket*, an engine made in the United States began to run on a short line from Charleston, South Carolina. The engine was named *The Best Friend of Charleston*. It pulled four loaded cars, very little cars they were, at the rate of sixteen miles an hour.

In 1831 the *Tom Thumb* made thirteen miles an hour on the Baltimore and Ohio Railroad; and the same year the *De Witt Clinton* ran seventeen miles an hour on a railroad in New York.

These first railroad engines were very odd-looking. They were shaped like some of our present-day road rolling machines. The first passenger cars were odder still. They were simply large stagecoaches. The wheels had special rims to keep them on the rails. Passengers could ride on top, if they liked, but they did so at the risk of being burned by the showering sparks from the engine.

The race of the cities.   Inventors learned how to make both engines and cars better and better. The Atlantic coast cities now pushed railroad building to the West. A little earlier they had raced for western trade by roads and canals. Now each large city tried to have a railroad line to the West. Railroads running north and south were also built. By 1850 there were nine thousand miles of railroads in the United States, and only ten years later there were more than thirty thousand miles.

How the railroads served the country.   Cities and towns sprang up along the railroads. New farms were cleared and cultivated, and the value of land rose rapidly. The railroads carried the crops of the farms to market in the cities, and took back to the farms the goods made in the city factories.

The railroads carried mail as well as freight. The government sent the mail by the fastest trains. Newspapers were carried cheaply, so that people could know promptly what was happening throughout the country. Travel increased. By carrying passengers, freight and mail, the railroads helped to educate the people.

THE MAGIC TELEGRAPH WIRES

Morse invents the telegraph. The discovery of a way to send messages over a wire by electricity was the work of Samuel F. B. Morse.

Morse was born in Massachusetts during Washington's first term as President of the United States. Like Robert Fulton, he grew up to be a portrait painter; and like Fulton again, his great idea came to him while he was on a trip to Europe. He returned to the United States and set to work.

He soon made instruments with which he could send messages a short distance. He was certain that with the same instruments he could send messages a long distance. But he had no money to buy miles of wire and stretch it on poles to prove what he could do.

He talked to wealthy men, and they shook their heads in pity or else made fun of what they considered his "hare-brained" ideas. Unlike Robert Livingston, who helped Fulton, they were not willing to risk any money on what seemed to them such a wild scheme.

Morse begs the government to help. But Morse would not give up. He knew that his instruments would work. He turned to Congress, and begged the government to put up a wire from Washington to Baltimore, forty miles away. If he could send messages forty miles, he could send them a thousand.

Morse set up his instruments in the Capitol, and

ticked off messages to an assistant in another room. Congressmen came and looked and heard the instruments ticking, and they went away telling each other that there might be something in the "old crank's" idea after all.   Anyway, they were willing to spend some of the government's money to test the scheme.

So finally Congress set aside thirty thousand dollars to be used in putting up the wire to Baltimore.   The line was finished in the spring of 1844 and worked just as well as the short wires had done.

The first important news sent by telegraph was a report of the Democratic National Convention in May, 1844.   This convention nominated Polk for the presidency, see page 109, and declared that our government must get the whole of Oregon and take Texas into the Union.

The rapid spread of telegraphy.   Morse was already fifty-three years old when the first telegram went over the wire from Baltimore to Washington.   Before he died he saw wires stretching from the Atlantic to the Pacific and from the Great Lakes to the Gulf of Mexico.   Four years before his death, a cable was laid under the waters of the Atlantic Ocean, and messages could be sent over it to England as quickly as over the wires from Baltimore to Washington.

Some useful effects of telegraphy.   To tell the whole story of how Morse's invention has changed our ways of living would fill a small book.   Only a few of the changes that it brought about can be mentioned here.

1. Railroad companies at once built telegraph lines along their roads, and began to run their trains by

telegraphic orders. A train dispatcher at headquarters would send orders to stations along the road, and the conductors and engineers would get the orders as their trains passed the stations. In this way the danger of accidents was greatly lessened and the train service was made much better.

2. Business men could send and receive orders for goods by telegraph, and could even manage their business by telegraph when absent from home. In this way business could be carried on with more speed and more profit than ever before.

3. The telegraph made possible the modern newspaper. With news traveling over the wires with the speed of light, daily papers could now tell their readers what was happening all over the world as soon as it happened.

4. The telegraph added greatly to **the happiness** of people by making it possible for them to keep in touch with their loved ones when absent from home.

The railroad and the telegraph. Railroad and telegraph made it possible for people to get what they wanted when they wanted it. The day of the ox-wagon, the stage coach, the canoe, and the sailboat was passing.

THE STORY OF THE SEWING MACHINE

Elias Howe invents the sewing machine. Until the very middle of the nineteenth century every stitch in the clothes that people wore had to be put in by hand.

Elias Howe, the inventor of the sewing machine, was born while Monroe was President. As a boy he worked on his father's farm and went to school in the little

Massachusetts village where he was born. When he was about eighteen years old he went to work in a factory which made nothing but machinery for cotton mills. Here, making the machines that made cloth, the idea came to the boy that there ought to be still another machine. There ought to be a machine to make cloth into clothes more quickly and easily than could be done by hand sewing.

For the next ten years Howe spent all his spare time and money trying to invent a sewing machine. At last, in 1845, he succeeded. He made a machine that would sew. That was just a year after the telegraph wires had first carried messages from Baltimore to Washington.

Now Howe had to go through the same sort of disappointment that Morse had suffered with his invention of the telegraph. He had no factory to make his sewing machines, and for a long time he could not find any factory owner who would undertake to make the machines for him.

Besides this disappointment, Howe found that the clothing makers did not want to use his machine. They feared that it would sew so fast that there would no longer be enough work to keep them all busy, and that a great many would find themselves out of work.

Finally the tide turned. By 1850 a few sewing machines were in use. Five years later several factories were making them and Howe was a rich man.

What the sewing machine did for women. The sewing machine was a great help to women. Families used to be much larger than they are now. A family with ten or fifteen children was not uncommon, and in such a

This early reaper is simple compared with a modern harvesting machine, but in your grandfather's day it seemed a marvelous invention.

family all the mother's time was taken up from sunrise until long after dark in cooking and sewing for the children. The sewing machine lessened and quickened her labor, and gave her a little time for pleasure and enjoyment.

CYRUS McCORMICK AND HIS REAPER

The Virginia home. In 1809 Cyrus Hall McCormick was born on a large farm in Rockbridge County, Virginia. A boy who liked to invent things could not have found a more interesting place in which to grow up than this farm, set in a green valley, with the peaks of the Blue Ridge Mountains on the east and those of the Alleghanies on the west. The McCormick home was more than a farm. Cyrus's father had two grist-mills, two saw-mills, an iron furnace, a woodworking shop, and a blacksmith shop.

The beginning of the reaper. When Cyrus McCormick was a boy, grain had to be cut by hand with a scythe or a cradle and laid on the ground. Then it was taken up and tied into bundles with wisps of the grain stalks. Hard back-breaking work it was, but it had to be done if people were to have bread. Cyrus did not like this hard work, and he began to wonder how it could be made easier. His father had tried to make a machine to do the work, but it was not successful. Cyrus then made some changes and improvements in it and was able to succeed where his father had failed.

The testing of the reaper. Before the young inventor finished his machine the harvest of 1831 was nearly all gathered. Only one small field had been left for the test, a golden field in the green valley over which rose the peaks of the Blue Ridge. Cyrus hitched a horse to the shafts and drove the machine into the over-ripe grain for the first test. "The wheel revolved and swept the gentle wheat downward upon the knife. Click! Click! Click! The white steel blade shot back and forth. The grain was cut."

The next year McCormick gave a public exhibition of his reaper. Many people came to see the strange machine work, some to make smart remarks and to predict its failure. The field was hilly and unsuited to the reaper; it rocked and jolted, and the owner rushed out and stopped the experiment, saying that his wheat was being ruined and wasted. The people were amused, and the young inventor must have been greatly discouraged.

Just at this moment a man came up and told McCormick to take the machine into his field, on the other side of the fence, and give it a fair test. This second field was level, and the reaper cut six acres of grain in one day! People now praised the machine, but none would buy it. It was *nine* years before anybody bought a McCormick reaper.

The first sale. Nine hard years they were for Cyrus McCormick. He became an iron manufacturer, but hard times ruined his business. He gave up his farm and all his property to his creditors. He did not give up the reaper, and probably no one would have taken it, even if he had offered to give it up.

In spare moments he worked away in the log blacksmith shop, always trying to make it a better reaper. Then one fine day, as the story often goes, a man rode up to the little log house and bought a reaper, paying fifty dollars for it. His name was Abraham Smith. The next year McCormick sold no reapers, but in 1842 he sold seven, the next year twenty-nine, and in 1844 he sold fifty.

The West used the reapers. Among the orders that came in 1844 seven were from the West; that is, from the land west of the mountains. These machines were sent by canal to Richmond, by river boat to the sea, then by ocean vessel to New Orleans, then up the Mississippi to Cincinnati, and from there by wagon to the places from which the orders came. Four of them arrived too late for the harvest, and two of them were never paid for! It was quite clear that something must be done if the reapers were to be used in the West. It took too long to ship them from Virginia.

Then came the great turning point in the life of Cyrus McCormick. A friend said, "Cyrus, why don't you go West with your Reaper, where *the land is level and labor is scarce?*"

Cyrus knew that his reaper could do good work on level land and that it saved labor. He put three hundred dollars in his money belt and set out on a three-thousand-mile journey which carried him through many states. Finally he came out of the timbered country into the level prairies of Illinois. He knew that here was the place for the reaper, and in 1847, with the help of William Butler Ogden, he built the reaper factory in Chicago. From then on he sold hundreds of reapers each year.

The work of the reaper. The reaper spread with the growth of wheat throughout the West, and over the world. It sped up harvesting so that more grain could be planted. It made the United States the leading wheat-producing nation of the world. It did away with the drudgery of swinging the scythe and cradle, and the toil of gathering the grain by hand and tying it by hand in the terrible summer heat. It made it possible for a few men with machines to provide bread for many more people than ever before.

It is said that Cyrus McCormick drove famine from

the world by enabling farmers to grow and gather enough wheat to make bread for everybody. That statement is not quite true, but he rendered the world a great service by making the scarcity of bread much less common. His invention made the world a better and safer place in which to live, and for that reason the inventor and his invention have a place in the history of the whole world where grain is grown.

A SHORT STORY TO TELL

For nearly two hundred years after the first settlers landed at Jamestown people lived year after year in much the same way. They traveled on horses and stagecoaches, in canoes and sailboats. Their mail was slow and uncertain. They had no factories and had to buy factory-made goods in Europe. Then the ways of living suddenly changed.

Robert Fulton invented the first successful steamboat in the world in 1807. Almost at the same time Americans began to build factories and make things by machinery. They dug canals and made better roads.

In 1830 the first steam engine began to run on an American railroad, and very soon after that railroads were spreading throughout the country.

All these inventions made it possible for people to travel more comfortably, and to send news and freight more rapidly and more cheaply than their fathers had done.

Then Morse invented telegraphy, and people could send messages over wires in the twinkling of an eye. Almost at the same time that Morse invented telegraphy, Elias Howe invented the sewing machine, and farmers began to harvest their grain with Cyrus Mc-Cormick's reaper.   In the short space of forty years steam, electricity, and machinery changed most of the old ways of living.

THINGS TO DO TOGETHER

1. Make a decorated border for your blackboard in which you draw pictures to show the changes in travel and in carrying messages and news.

2. Appoint a bulletin-board committee to sort and mount pictures, which the class will bring, to show how inventions have made our ways of living better.   Write sentences under the pictures to tell why they were chosen.

3. Appoint a committee to show how the miles of railroad have increased.   Use a line one-half inch long to show one thousand miles.   Draw a line from left to right on the blackboard to show the number of miles of railroad in the United States in 1850.   Under this line draw one to show the number of miles of railroad in 1860.   Find out how many miles of railroad there are today and draw a third line to show the miles today.

PICTURE STORIES

4. Choose one of the pictures in this chapter and tell to the class the story that the picture tells you.

5. Read in other books, stories of the inventors told about in this chapter.   Write the story you found most interesting, and if you like to draw, illustrate the story with your drawings.

UNIT THREE

THE NATION EXPANDS TO THE PACIFIC

By the purchase of Louisiana President Jefferson carried the western boundary of the United States to the Rocky Mountains. Curious to learn all he could about the new territory, the President sent two young army officers, Meriwether Lewis and William Clark, to explore the Missouri River to its head. Then they crossed the mountains and went down the Columbia River to the Pacific Ocean. About the same time another young officer, Lieutenant Zebulon Pike, was exploring the plains and mountains further south. Lewis and Clark and Pike made maps and wrote books, telling about the nature of the country that they explored.

By traveling down the Columbia River to the ocean, Lewis and Clark gave the United States a right to claim all the Oregon country, and a few years later emigrants began to move there and build homes.

Meantime hundreds of families had gone to Texas, which then belonged to Mexico. Each family received more than four thousand acres of land. After a few years the colonists in Texas grew tired of the rule of Mexico, declared their independence, and became part of the United States.

The Mexican government continued to claim Texas. The quarrel grew into war, and in the end, the United States took California and New Mexico and paid the Mexican government fifteen million dollars.

Thus the United States moved its western boundary to the Pacific Ocean. Rich gold mines were discovered in California just about that time, and the next year more than a hundred thousand people went there to live.

BOOKS YOU WILL ENJOY FOR UNIT THREE

Bass, Florence, *Stories of Early Times in the Great West* (The Bobbs-Merrill Company).

Hunt, R. D., *California, a Little History of a Big State* (D. C. Heath and Company).

Ginnell, G. B., *Jack Among the Indians* (Frederick A. Stokes Company).

Standing Bear, Luther, *Stories of the Sioux* (Houghton, Mifflin Company).

Barstow, C. L., *The Westward Movement* (D. Appleton-Century Company).

Snedden, G. S., *Docas, the Indian Boy of Santa Clara* (D. C. Heath and Company).

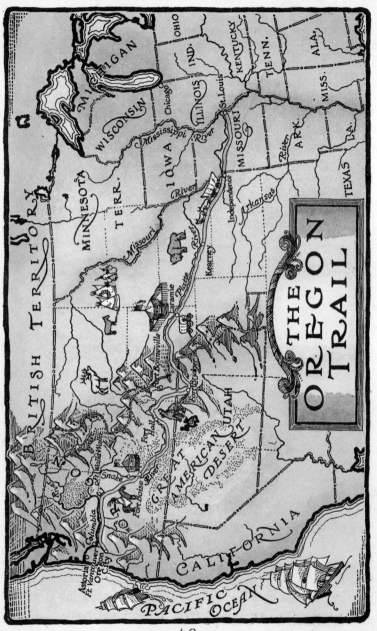

THE OREGON TRAIL

Chapter IX

THE ROAD TO OREGON

Daniel Boone

THE WESTWARD MOVEMENT

New states come into the Union. While Washington was President three new states came into the Union— Vermont, Kentucky, and Tennessee. Two of the three, Kentucky and Tennessee, lie west of the Appalachian Mountains. Another western state, Ohio, came into the Union in 1803, while Jefferson was President. Louisiana and Indiana came into the Union while Madison was President. Mississippi, Illinois, Alabama, Maine, and Missouri, came in under Monroe. Thus, the Union had grown to twenty-four states when Jackson became President.

The admission of these new states to the Union meant that people had moved into them from the old

(97)

states, driven out the Indians, and built their homes in the forest.

The settlement of America like a moving picture. The story of the settlement of the United States is much like a moving picture. In the first reel we see the settlers arrive from Europe in their queer-looking ships. They unload their chests and trunks; the ships sail away. They build log cabins, clear land, and plant their crops. And always they are in danger of their lives from the tomahawk and scalping knife of Indians on the warpath.

The next reel shows hunters pushing into the forests, hunting deer and bears and panthers. They want the skins for clothing and rugs and bedding. Following the hunters come men and women and children, leaving the old settlements by the sea to make new homes in the western woods.

We see them on the trail, sometimes in wagons, sometimes walking. Their long rifles are on their shoulders, and perhaps all the family's belongings are in a pack on one shaggy horse.

They select a wooded hilltop near the bank of a running stream. Out come the axes. Trees are felled, a little field is cleared, and almost in the twinkling of an eye, smoke is rising from the cabin chimneys and corn is growing in the clearings. Always the movement is toward the west, and always the Indians are near, with tomahawk, knife, and torch.

So the picture moves on; up the rivers; across the Appalachian Mountains; across the broad Mississippi; across the high, dry plains of the West; across the

Rocky Mountains; and finally to the shores of the rolling Pacific. The last picture is the United States.

The movement across the continent. The westward march of pioneers never stopped. Always a line of restless frontiersmen like Daniel Boone were seeking "elbow room" farther west. Loading their few household goods on a pack-horse or two, shouldering their rifles, and whistling their dogs around them, they would leave their cabins empty and trudge farther into the woods.

Behind the frontiersmen came another line, pushing into the cabins and little clearings which the frontiersmen left vacant. This second line was made up of men and women and children who had come to stay. They made the cabins larger and more comfortable; they widened their small clearings; and settled down to "grow up with the country."

The movement went on continuously like waves on the sea-shore. Each new wave carried the pioneers a little farther westward. The permanent settlers would come up on the heels of the frontier hunters and trappers and the frontiersmen would move farther west. Then another wave of settlers would crowd them and they would move again.

FUR TRADERS AND MISSIONARIES

Fur traders lead the way to Oregon. By the time that Andrew Jackson became President (in 1829), the Westward Movement had carried the line of settlements beyond the Mississippi River. Where could the frontiersmen, the trappers and the fur traders go next?

Frontiersmen going westward loaded their household goods on
pack-horses and traveled across prairies and through forests. They
found traveling difficult, for there were no roads anywhere and no
bridges over the streams.

Their eyes had long been turned to the Far Northwest,
to the Oregon country, that distant land which President Jefferson had sent Lewis and Clark to explore,
and which they had praised so highly.

In all the United States, the man most keenly interested in the Lewis and Clark expedition was President Jefferson. Next to him, perhaps, was John Jacob
Astor, a farsighted merchant of New York City, who
came to the United States from Germany about the
time the War for Independence was ended.

When Astor read the reports of Lewis and Clark he formed a plan to build a fur-trading house at the mouth of the Columbia River. He carried out his plan and named the settlement that he made there Astoria.

Astor gave up his settlement at Astoria during the War of 1812. When the war was over he did not go on with his plans, but other trappers visited the Oregon country and told of its beauties. They described it as a

About 1840 the Methodist church established a mission at the Dalles on the Columbia River.

wonderful country with a fine climate and fertile lands, with lofty mountains and green valleys, with great forests and running streams filled with game and fish.

Here was a glorious country! The stories of Oregon set the blood of old frontiersmen dancing in their veins. Boone, on the very edge of western settlement in Missouri, heard the tales, and his old heart ached to take the trail to the distant land that seemed more beautiful than Kentucky had seemed in his youth. Death stopped the wanderings of Boone, but the fur traders continued to bring back their tales. They were preparing the way for the settlement of Oregon.

Missionaries follow the fur traders. While Andrew Jackson was President, some Indians from Oregon came to St. Louis and asked for missionaries to come and teach them the white man's "Book of Heaven," the Bible.

In answer to their prayer, the Methodist Church sent out to Oregon the Rev. Jason Lee, accompanied by his wife, his nephew, and several others. The next year the Presbyterian Church sent Dr. Marcus Whitman to build a mission. These two churches were the beginning of the American settlement of Oregon.

Settlers follow the missionaries. After spending a few years in Oregon, Lee returned to New York, and all the way across Illinois, Indiana, and Ohio he talked to people about the delightful climate and the wonderful farming land of Oregon. The newspapers began to publish stories about Oregon. Very soon people began to talk of going to Oregon.

Nearly a hundred emigrants went out in 1842. The

next spring a great party collected at Independence, Missouri, ready to "jump off" as soon as the snow melted.

Marcus Whitman guides the emigrants to Oregon. It happened that Marcus Whitman had been to New York during the winter on business for his church and was returning in the spring to Oregon. He had already crossed the continent four times, twice each way, and knew the best route. When the leaders of the emigrants learned that he was at Independence in the spring of 1843, they asked him to guide the party.

Whitman was glad to lead the travelers, for he wanted to see Oregon settled. He had long believed it possible to open a wagon road all the way to Oregon, and here was his chance to prove it. He did prove it, and the next year a larger party of settlers went to Oregon, with only covered wagons for travel and shelter.

SCENES ON THE OREGON TRAIL

The start. Francis Parkman, a great historian and a charming writer, once made a trip half way to Oregon and wrote a book which he called the *Oregon Trail*. In it he told of how the emigrants traveled to the Oregon country, and of the various things that happened on the way.

Parkman first describes the scene at Independence, Missouri, just before the spring "jump off" for Oregon began:

"There was a great hammering and banging from a dozen blacksmiths' sheds, where the heavy wagons were being repaired, and the horses and oxen shod.

Most of the westward-bound pioneers made the long, hard trip across the continent in covered wagons drawn by oxen. Because there were no stores or inns along the way they had to carry all the provisions that they needed and to prepare their own food.

The streets were filled with men, horses and mules. While I was in town, a train of wagons from Illinois passed through, to join the camp in the prairie, and stopped in the main street.

"Dozens of healthy children's faces were peeping from under the covers of the wagons. Here and there a girl was seated on horseback, holding over her sunburnt face an old umbrella or a parasol, once gaudy enough, but now much faded. The men, very sober looking countrymen, stood about their oxen."

The Kansas Indians. Parkman describes a visit that he received from an old Kansas Indian:

"Scarcely were we seated when a visitor came up. This was an old Kansas Indian. His head was shaved and painted red, and from the tuft of hair remaining on the crown dangled several eagle's feathers and the tails of two or three rattlesnakes. His cheeks, too, were covered with red paint, his ears were adorned with green glass earrings. A collar of grizzly-bears' claws hung around his neck, and several large necklaces of wampum hung on his breast.

"Having shaken us by the hand with a grunt, the old man, dropping his red blanket from his shoulders, sat down crosslegged on the ground. We offered him a cup of sweetened water, at which he said "Good." He was beginning to tell us how great a man he was, and how many Pawnees he had killed, when a strange looking crowd appeared wading the creek towards us.

"They filed past in rapid succession, men, women, and children: some were on horseback, some on foot. Old squaws, mounted astride of shaggy, thin little ponies, with perhaps one or two snake-eyed children seated behind them, clinging to their tattered blankets; tall, lank young men on foot, with bows and arrows in their hands; and girls that not even the charms of glass beads and scarlet cloth could make pretty, made up the procession. They were the outcasts of the Kansas nation, on a begging trip."

From such Indians there was nothing to fear but thievery, but those the emigrants met on the trail were of a very different sort.

The covered wagon. Emerson Hough (Huff), a story writer who knew the West and loved it, has told of the long trip to Oregon in his book *The Covered Wagon*.

Breaking camp in the morning. At the break of dawn the sleeping camp was awakened by rifle shots or a bugle call. The cooks began getting breakfast ready, and the night guards brought in the horses, oxen, and cattle. By six o'clock the teams were hitched and the wagons were packed, ready for the signal of the leader to go.

On the trail. On the trail the wagons dragged out into a line sometimes a mile long. Scouts armed with rifles and pistols rode in front and at each side, to guard against surprise by Indians. Hunting parties rode off from time to time and brought in fresh buffalo, elk, or deer meat to vary the regular fare of dried beef, bacon, coffee, and bread.

The night camp. At night the wagons were "parked" in a circle to form a barricade, and the camp was pitched within the circle. The horses and oxen were hobbled, guards were posted, and the tired travelers slept.

Week after week and month after month they traveled on in this way, while the slow ox-wagons creaked and jolted across the prairies of Missouri and Iowa, the plains of Nebraska, and the bleak mountain passes of Wyoming and Idaho into Oregon. Starting in May, a party, with good luck, could reach the lower Columbia Valley sometime in November.

Dr. John McLoughlin helps the new settlers. The first emigrants would have had a hard time before they could raise grain and vegetables but for the help of Dr. John McLoughlin. He was the manager of the British Hudson's Bay Fur Company in Oregon. He sold the settlers supplies on credit from the company's store houses, and sometimes let his Indian laborers work for them.

THE UNITED STATES AND ENGLAND BOTH CLAIM OREGON

Why the United States claimed Oregon. The United States claimed the Oregon country for four reasons:

1. Captain Robert Gray, an American sea captain, discovered the Columbia River in 1792.

2. Lewis and Clark explored and made maps of the country in 1805–1806.

3. John Jacob Astor established Astoria in 1811, and American fur traders continued to visit the country after the War of 1812.

4. By the Florida Treaty of 1819 Spain gave up to the United States all its claims to the country.

Why England claimed Oregon. England also claimed the country for four reasons:

1. Sir Francis Drake had taken possession of the whole Pacific coast in the name of Queen Elizabeth in 1579.

2. Captain James Cook, another Englishman, explored the Oregon coast in 1778, two hundred years after Drake.

3. Lieutenant George Vancouver, of the English navy, explored the Columbia River in 1792, just after Gray discovered it.

4. English trappers and fur traders were already in the country when Astor established Astoria, and remained there after the War of 1812.

The settlers gain Oregon for the United States. Which nation had the better right to Oregon? The question

"FIFTY-FOUR FORTY OR FIGHT"
The territory claimed by the United States in the cry, "Fifty-four Forty or Fight." (Note the present northern boundary of the U.S.

was of little importance so long as the country was unsettled. But when American settlers began to pour into the country by thousands, as they did every year after 1843, it became necessary to decide the question promptly and to set up a government in Oregon.

First the United States offered to divide the Oregon country, but England would not agree to the line that our government offered and both countries continued to claim the territory.

By 1844 the people of the United States were determined to have a settlement of the Oregon question. When the Democrats nominated James K. Polk for the presidency, they took as their campaign war cry: "All Oregon or none; Fifty-four forty or fight!" The meaning of this statement was that the Democrats claimed the territory as far north as 54° 40′, which, as you will notice on the map, is far up toward Alaska.

And the Democrats won! Polk was elected. England now made an offer. It offered to run the boundary along the forty-ninth parallel of latitude, giving the present states of Oregon and Washington to the United States. The Senate advised President Polk to accept the English offer, which he did. The treaty which settled the matter was signed at Washington in 1846.

The United States now stretched from the Atlantic to the Pacific. The Westward Movement had carried the American people from ocean to ocean, and still the trails to the West were crowded. In 1860, fifteen years after the dispute with England was settled, there were more than fifty thousand people in Oregon.

A SHORT STORY TO TELL

You remember that President Jefferson sent Lewis and Clark to explore the territory of Louisiana and the country west of the Rocky Mountains. After they returned, trappers and fur traders began to go into the country to trap animals and buy skins from the Indians.

The northern country west of the mountains was called Oregon.

Both England and the United States claimed Oregon, and it seemed for a while that England would get it. But Englishmen did not go to Oregon to open farms, make homes, and rear families; they went only to hunt and trade. The Americans went to stay. First the Methodist and Presbyterian churches sent missionaries to teach the Indians. Then, after a few years, long trains of covered wagons began to carry American families across the Great Plains and the Rocky Mountains. American farmers began to spread over the country, and from that moment it was certain that the United States would win.

In 1846 the United States and England signed a treaty, or agreement. The treaty gave the United States all the land that now makes up the states of Oregon and Washington.

MEN OF IMPORTANCE

1. Write sentences telling what each of these men did in connection with the Oregon territory.

Marcus Whitman	John Jacob Astor
Dr. John McLoughlin	Robert Gray
James Cook	Francis Parkman
George Vancouver	Jason Lee

ADVERTISING OREGON

2. Write an advertisement for the Oregon country. Use a geography to find more information about the soil, the climate, and the natural resources. When the advertisements are completed, read them to the class.

THINGS TO DO

Choose one of the activities listed below.

3. Make a poster advertising Oregon.

4. Make a number of pictures that will show the settlement of America as it is described on page 98.

5. Make a map of the western part of the United States and show on it the Oregon trail. Mark places of importance along the trail such as the place of the "jump off," the forts, and the chief rivers that were followed. Mark the 49th parallel which was the final boundary between the United States and Canada.

6. Act out a play which will tell of a day's experiences on the Oregon trail. Perhaps everyone in the class can take part in the play.

7. Tell a story about one of the pictures in this chapter.

3rd, six weeks

Chapter X

THE UNITED STATES GETS TEXAS

Stephen F. Austin

THE AMERICANS SETTLE TEXAS

Moses Austin leads the Westward Movement to Texas.
Moses Austin of Missouri formed the plan that led to
the settlement of Texas by Americans. In 1820, with
one servant, a negro, he set out for Texas, which then
belonged to Spain. At San Antonio, Texas, he asked
if he might bring his own and three hundred other
families to Texas. He was told that he might, and also
get land for them, but before he could do so, he died.

Stephen F. Austin carries out his father's plan. Stephen
F. Austin settled nearly a thousand families in Texas.
His work was like that of Lord Baltimore and William
Penn and Oglethorpe in settling Maryland, Pennsyl-
vania, and Georgia. And his work was very important.

The many rivers flowing west and south were favorite highways
for settlers seeking new homes in the Southwest.

The settlement of Americans in Texas not only brought
Texas finally into the United States, but led to the
United States' getting also New Mexico, Arizona, California, Nevada, Utah, Colorado, and the southern part
of Wyoming.

Settlers came to Texas from all the states of the
Union, but most of them were from the South and
West—from Louisiana, Mississippi, Alabama, Tennes-
see and Missouri.

The easy way to Texas. It was not so hard to get to
Texas as it was later to get to Oregon and California.

Texas was not so far off, and the broad, swift current of the Mississippi River took travelers almost all of the way there.

Emigrants, as the people bound for the West were called, would load a flatboat on the Ohio, the Tennessee, or the Cumberland and float comfortably down to New Orleans. From New Orleans a swift-sailing ship could land them in Texas in three or four days. Many followed this easy way. Others traveled in covered wagons, the same way that the emigrants went by the northern route to Oregon.

Early hardships. The hardships of the first settlers in Texas were very great. There were only two small villages of civilized Mexican people in Texas. Indians roamed over the rest of the country. For the first few years the settlers suffered terribly at the hands of the Indians.

Then, drouth dried up their crops one year and overflows from the rivers drowned them the next. The crops failed, and sometimes the people had nothing to eat but lean deer and mustang horses. Somehow they managed to live. Other colonists arrived, and Texas was soon the home of many thousand men, women and children like those who lived in Missouri and Arkansas. But in those days Texas did not belong to the United States. It belonged to Mexico, which had gained its independence from Spain in 1821.

Why American settlers went to Texas. Americans went to Texas for the same reason that Daniel Boone went to Kentucky, and then to Missouri. The desire of the West was in their blood. They longed for new scenes. They wanted new land. Mexico gave every family four thousand acres of land. And such land! The settlers boasted that there was none better in all the world.

Just as Mexico opened Texas with its fine, free land, hard times struck the United States. Many families in the great Mississippi Valley lost all they had. They lost their farms, cattle, horses, the very roofs that covered their heads. They wanted a new start, but at home there was no chance. The United States government did not give its land away. It wanted to sell its land, sell it for cash; and they had no cash. Is it strange that they went to Texas?

THE AMERICAN SETTLERS MAKE TEXAS INDEPENDENT

President Santa Anna forces the Texans into war. The settlers went to Texas with thankful hearts for the gift of so much land by the Mexican government, but in 1835 President Santa Anna overthrew the republican government of Mexico, and made himself dictator, or king, of Mexico.

The settlers declared that they wanted no king to rule them, so they drove all Santa Anna's troops from Texas. But the next year Santa Anna brought his Mexican soldiers back again, an army of five thousand men.

The fall of the Alamo. With half his army, on March 6, 1836, Santa Anna stormed the Alamo, at San Antonio. The Alamo was the ruined chapel of an old Spanish mission, or church, which the Texans had made into a fort. It was defended by about two hun-

In the battle of the Alamo a small force of Texans defended themselves against many times their own number of Mexican troops until not a Texan was left alive.

dred men, commanded by William B. Travis and James Bowie. David Crockett, the famous Tennessee hunter and humorist, had joined them with his violin and his faithful rifle, "Betsy."

On February 24, 1836, Travis sent out a call for help "To the People of Texas and all Americans in the World: I am besieged by a thousand or more of the Mexicans under Santa Anna. *I shall never surrender or retreat.* I am determined to sustain myself as long as possible and die like a soldier who never forgets what is due to his own honor and that of his country. Victory or death."

President Theodore Roosevelt described the battle at the Alamo as one of the bravest fights ever carried on by fearless men. All the men knew that they would certainly be killed, but they said that they would rather die than give up the fort. They were killed to the very last man.

Americans of every state and for all time may well be proud of the courage and love of duty which the Alamo stands for. The old stone building, now in the center of the rushing city of San Antonio, is a monument to one of the most heroic acts in the whole of American history.

Three weeks after the fall of the Alamo, another part of the army of Santa Anna captured and put to death by his orders nearly four hundred men who had just come from the United States to aid the Texans.

General Houston wins the independence of Texas. Santa Anna's victories made him reckless. Leaving his main army, he swept eastward rapidly with eleven or twelve hundred men. He intended to end the war at a blow. He met General Sam Houston with eight hundred Texans in the Battle of San Jacinto, and lost his whole force. Six hundred Mexicans were killed at San Jacinto and the rest were captured.

Santa Anna himself was captured, and came to an agreement with Houston. He agreed to order his main army back to Mexico and to give up Texas, letting it be free from Mexico. And free Texas has remained, though Mexico still claimed it for ten years longer.

THE UNITED STATES TAKES TEXAS INTO THE UNION

England has its eye on Texas. President Tyler came to believe in 1843 that England was about to get possession of the Republic of Texas. He believed that it would be harmful to the United States for England to hold Texas. In order to keep England from getting it, he offered to take Texas into the Union and make it a part of the United States.

As most of the Texans had gone to Texas from the United States, they wanted to be taken in again and were delighted with President Tyler's offer. It took some time to carry out the plan, however, and Texas did not get into the Union until December, 1845.

Texas was a vast territory in the Southwest. It added to the United States half as much territory as the Louisiana Purchase. One more step was still necessary to round out the map of the United States to its present form and make it look as it does today. The next chapter tells how the United States got the rest of its territory.

A SHORT STORY TO TELL

American settlers began to go to Texas before the first missionaries went to Oregon to teach the Indians the "White man's book of Heaven." Texas belonged to Mexico, but the Mexicans wanted people from the United States and Europe to settle in their country and offered free land to all who would come.

Stephen F. Austin, of Missouri, led the first settlers to Texas. The early pioneers had a hard time in the new country. But more and more families came from the United States and opened farms and cattle ranches, and after a few years the hard times passed.

Just as the settlers were becoming comfortable and happy, President Santa Anna set himself up as dictator, or king, of Mexico. The American settlers would not have Santa Anna for their ruler and declared themselves independent of Mexico. Santa Anna then led a Mexican army to Texas to compel the Texans to remain under the Mexican government. At first he was successful in all the battles, but in the Battle of San Jacinto General Sam Houston captured Santa Anna and won the independence of Texas. In 1845 the United States took Texas into the Union.

STORY RELAY

1. Let ten members of the class each choose one of the names in the list below. Let these pupils tell the story of Texas in relay, beginning with the story of the first person in the list.

LaSalle	William Travis
De Vaca	James Bowie
Moses Austin	David Crockett
Stephen Austin	Sam Houston
Santa Anna	John Tyler

SHOWING IT ON THE MAP

2. On a map show how it was easier to go to Texas than to Oregon.

3. On a map point out the territories that were added to the original United States and tell something about each territory.

JUST IMAGINE

4. Pretend you are one of the early settlers in Texas. Write a letter to a friend telling of the hardships and dangers of your life in this newly settled land.

5. Imagine that you are David Crockett and tell some of the experiences you have had on your travels with "Betsy." For more information about Crockett read, *Four American Pioneers* by F. M. Perry and K. Beebe (American Book Company) pages 135–194.

Hand-to-hand fighting between the Americans and the Mexicans during the War with Mexico

Chapter XI

THE UNITED STATES GETS CALIFORNIA AND THE FAR SOUTHWEST

James K. Polk

THE WAR WITH MEXICO

Mexico refuses to give up Texas. Though the Republic of Texas had been independent for nine years when the United States took it into the Union, Mexico objected to its joining the United States. The Mexican government claimed that Texas still belonged to Mexico, and that the United States had done Mexico a great injury by taking the territory.

Mexico refuses to pay damages to American citizens. At the same time American business men and ship-owners doing business in Mexico claimed that wars and revolutions in Mexico had hurt their business, and said that the Mexican government ought to repay their losses. But the Mexican government did nothing for them.

President Polk tries to settle with Mexico. Finally President Polk made up his mind that Mexico must settle these American claims one way or another. It must either pay them, or it must examine them and give its reasons for not paying them.

Polk sent John Slidell of Louisiana to Mexico City. Mexico refused to receive Slidell or to talk about the claims of our citizens. It said that the United States must first settle with Mexico for taking Texas. After that important matter was out of the way, Mexico might be willing to talk about the matter of money claimed by American citizens.

This stand taken by the Mexican government really meant war. A Mexican army moved northward to the Rio Grande, and then crossed that river. An American army moved southward toward the Rio Grande. On April 26, 1846, scout parties of two armies fought a skirmish, and several American soldiers were killed.

When President Polk learned of the fighting he asked Congress to declare war against Mexico, and Congress passed the declaration on May 12, 1846.

The Mexican War. The war lasted a year and ten months. General Zachary Taylor led an American army southward from Texas and captured Monterey. General Winfield Scott landed an army at Vera Cruz and fought his way to Mexico City, which he captured in September, 1847. In the meantime, another military force took New Mexico, and a combined naval and land force took California.

The treaty of peace. The peace was signed in February, 1848. President Polk said that Mexico had forced the war upon the United States and must therefore pay the cost of the war. Since Mexico had no money, he would take California, which he wanted anyway, and all the rest of the territory west of Texas.

The territory taken from Mexico has since been formed into six states, New Mexico, Arizona, California, Nevada, Utah, and Colorado. This great amount of land seemed a little too much to take for the cost of the war, so the United States agreed to pay Mexico fifteen million dollars.

THE SETTLEMENT OF CALIFORNIA

The gold rush. A few days before Mexico signed the treaty that gave California to the United States, some workmen in California who were digging a ditch discovered gold at Sutter's Mill, on the American River.

Eight months later the eastern newspapers published the news. It had taken the story all that time to cross the continent. At once there was a bustle and stir from Maine to Texas and from the shore of the Atlantic to the Mississippi River.

Some men started immediately, determined to get to California before all the gold was picked up. Others made plans more carefully and got ready to start the next spring. Everywhere there was great excitement. Then, in the spring (1849), such a "gold rush" began as had never before been seen.

Soon after news of the discovery of gold in California reached the East, thousands of eager gold seekers made their way across the prairies and mountains to the gold fields.

The California trails. The "Forty-niners," as these first gold hunters were called, went to California by many different trails or routes, but there were four routes that were more popular than any others.

The quickest way, if one had good luck, was to go by ship to the Isthmus of Panama, cross the narrow neck of land on foot or mule-back, and catch a boat on the other side for San Francisco. But one must be lucky on this trip! Yellow fever lurked in the swamps of the Isthmus; and there might be no boat on the other side. In spite of the chances of death and delay, however, many followed this dangerous southern route by way of Panama. Most of them were daring young men, willing to risk their lives for a little more speed.

Another route followed the Oregon Trail to the Mormon settlement at the Great Salt Lake in Utah. There it turned southward through Nevada to California. Captain John C. Fremont, who had explored the mountains of California and Nevada for many years, had helped to open up this trail.

Still another route to the gold fields of California followed the Santa Fé Trail from Independence, Mis-

TRAILS USED BY EMIGRANTS TO WESTWARD LANDS ABOUT 1850

souri, to Santa Fé, New Mexico. From Santa Fé the way led down to the Mexican border, then across to southern California, and northward to Los Angeles.

> "It wound (this trail) through strange scarred hills, down canyons lone
> Where wild things screamed, with winds for company;
> Its mile-stones were the bones of pioneers.
> Bronzed, haggard men, often with thirst a-moan,
> Lashed on their beasts of burden toward the sea."

The popular southern route went through Texas. Several trails came together at El Paso, Texas, and passed then across New Mexico and Arizona to Los Angeles. *126 - 135*

Life on the southern trail. Sometimes a traveler took the trouble to keep a diary, telling day by day the happenings of the journey. Here are some extracts from the diary of Cornelius Cox, a young man who traveled by the southern route through Texas, New Mexico, and Arizona:

"We arrived at the crossing of the Rio Grande on the nineteenth of July. The river at this place is about one hundred and fifty yards wide, swift, muddy, and swimming from bank to bank.

"We used our boat and had everything ferried across by the twenty-third. The same evening we moved five miles up the river to Rattlesnake Camp. We stopped at this place to do some blacksmith work, but stayed longer than we expected.

"The thing that caused the delay was the reorganization of our party. Some of our company left us and went on ahead. They objected to traveling with our slow ox-teams. We were sorry to lose them.

"Yesterday we dined upon roast venison, turtle soup, and rolled dumpling. This morning we had milk toast for breakfast. The bread we now use is made from wheat, ground upon a steel mill. Flour was not to be had at El Paso, so we bought a mill and grind the wheat as we need it.

"There is one young lady with our company, a Miss Wayland from western Texas. She is about sixteen and quite a pretty girl. I have claimed kinship with her mother, whose maiden name was Cox, but she refuses to acknowledge me unless I will shave, which is a condition I cannot comply with.

"Cook's Springs, August 14: We are kept here today on account of the sickness of one of the company. He belonged to a small party that joined us on the road. One night he and his companions were attacked by a wolf, and before they could kill it, it had bitten six of the men. The wolf was believed to be mad, and the man who is now sick has strong symptoms of hydrophobia.

"The second day after leaving the river the company was thrown into great confusion and alarm by the appearance of an Indian. I had gone ahead with three others to explore the road and find a good campground. The wagons were strung along the road for about two miles, ox-teams in the rear.

"The Indian rode up to the leading wagons and said that there were a great many Apaches over the hills. Just then one of the men with me discharged his gun, and the company, hearing the report, believed that we were attacked.

"The news went to the rear, and a man there fired his gun to put a fresh load in it. This caused those in front to believe that the rear was attacked.

"Orders were promptly given for the train to close up, and for every man to be in readiness. I am told that such whipping and yelling of teamsters, such screaming of women and children, and such fuss and trouble generally never happened before, and all because of one poor Indian.

"There seems to have been a great deal of travel on this road. At every camp we see broken wagons, various articles of plunder, and the bones of oxen. I do not believe, however, that our party has lost even twenty-five cents worth of property on the road."

Cox was much amused by the dress of the Indians that he saw in Arizona. He wrote in his diary:

"The California travel has made a great change in the habits and dress of these Indians. They used to wear only a cloth around the waist. But how changed! You rarely see one now who is not wearing a shirt, a coat, or a pair of pants, but never a whole suit of clothes.

"I was much amused at one who came into our camp the first day. He had a high stove-pipe hat on his head and wore a heavy blue blanket coat all buttoned up to the chin. This, I suppose, was all he had on, for his legs and feet were bare. The perspiration poured from his face and head in streams, and he seemed fit to die of the heat. But he was very proud of the costume that made him so uncomfortable."

Panning dirt or gravel, especially that found near streams, was a common way of searching for gold in the early days of the gold rush. The lighter sands were washed off, leaving the heavier gold dust and nuggets in the bottom of the pan.

Cox left Houston, Texas, in April, 1849, and was eight months getting to Los Angeles. The same trip is made now on comfortable trains in forty-eight hours.

Life on the northern trail. Many thousands of travelers went by the northern route. Like the Oregon emigrants, they went during the early spring to St. Joseph or Independence, Missouri. When the spring grass along the trail was high enough to feed the horses, mules, and oxen which must pull the wagons to California, the gold seekers would "jump off" on the long, hard journey. The trail led across Nebraska, Wyoming, Utah, and Nevada, keeping always as near a stream as possible.

At the beginning, when men and teams were fresh and strong, traveling over the grass covered plains was delightful. But as week followed week and month followed month the trail became harder, and men wondered why they had ever started. Teams broke down and wagons had to be left behind.

Sometimes those who had bad luck were selfish and mean; sometimes they were generous and good. The mean ones tried to destroy what they left behind. They broke up the wagons, poured turpentine on the sugar, mixed salt and dirt with the flour, and destroyed the bacon. Since they could no longer carry the things with them, they did not want anybody else to use them. Sometimes, however, a traveler found wagons standing by the roadside with signs on them telling everybody who needed things to help themselves. These wagons were left by the good and generous men.

We have already seen how a traveler on the southern trail described his journey. Some of those on the northern trail, also, wrote diaries and letters telling what they saw and did. Here are parts of a diary written by a traveler from Pennsylvania. He started from Independence the first of May, 1850:

"*Tuesday, May 14.* Rolled out at half past seven. Found the roads very dusty. The road is filled with emigrants. We can count one hundred wagons ahead and behind us. We had one bad accident today. One of our teams ran around and broke the wagon tongue. All stopped, and in twenty minutes we had it so well mended that the team drove on and I think the tongue will stand for some days.

"We passed a fresh-made grave today. The head board stated the age of the dead man to be twenty-one, name Robert Malone. Many such accidents happen on the plains. I hope our company will not meet with such an accident. I think this lesson will have a good effect, by making all emigrants more careful with their guns. Report says no grass ahead. I hope it is not true.

"*Saturday, May 18, 1850.* We were all up early for a start, but we found that a mule of Black's was lost. One hour's search found the lost animal. We left camp at eight. Drove on rapidly.

"We saw four Indians today. They belonged to the Pawnee tribe, the first we have seen of this tribe. They are treacherous and savage, but they appeared very friendly. All they wished was tobacco and some other things, such as knives. They are noted cowards, but if they get you in their power, your situation is dangerous. I suppose ten men well armed could drive five hundred of them.

"*Friday, May 31, 1850.* We had an early start this morning. Found the roads sandy most of the time. The wagons run very heavy. The road is lined with emigrants, both before and behind our wagons. The horse teams are passing us. I hope they will hold out, but fear they will not. We passed a number of Indian wigwams today, I suppose they number thirty in one place. The Indians are of the Sioux tribe, quite good looking for red men. I got some buffalo meat from them and cooked it for supper this evening. I had some curiosity to taste the meat of this wild animal. Found it most delicious. I never ate better. We are getting on finely. Came twenty-two miles today.

"*Sunday, July 18, in Nevada.* We drove out early. Our mules almost gave out. We have now traveled

In the early days of California the miner usually paid for his provisions with gold dust or nuggets. The storekeeper often acted as banker for his customers.

three days with little or no feed. Our mules look badly. You will sometimes see twenty and thirty dead animals in two or three miles. Came twelve miles today."*

*Adapted from *A Pioneer of 1850,* copyrighted by Little, Brown & Company.

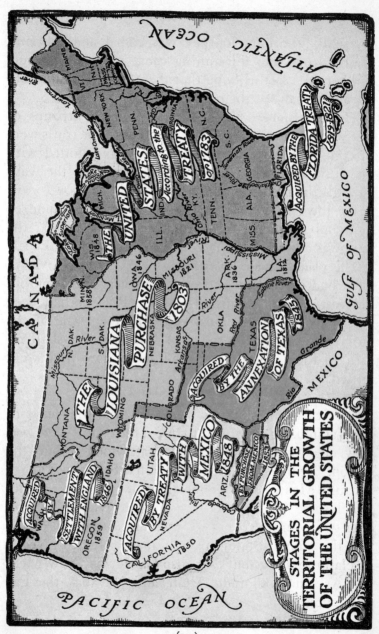

STAGES IN THE TERRITORIAL GROWTH OF THE UNITED STATES

Finally the long journey was ended and the emigrants drove into the mining camp near Sacramento, California.   Let us hope that they found enough gold to repay them for the hard trip.

The Forty-niners fill California.   Endless streams of emigrants poured across the continent.   The trails were littered with the skeletons of horses and dotted with the graves of men and women who died on the way; but still the rush went on.

By the end of 1849 there were nearly a hundred thousand people in California, and the next year the state was admitted to the Union.

The plains remain unsettled.   The Westward Movement had carried the settlers from ocean to ocean, but the vast, rolling plains east of the Rockies had been passed over.   The plains were still the home of the buffalo and of roving tribes of Indians.   We shall return to them before long and learn how they were settled.

A SHORT STORY TO TELL

Mexico would not give up Texas after the Battle of San Jacinto. It continued to claim the country and was very angry when the United States took it into the Union. At the same time the United States was angry because Mexico would not agree to pay for injuries which some American citizens had received in Mexico. The two countries went to war, and at the end of the war the United States not only made Mexico give up its claim to Texas but took also California, New Mexico, Arizona, Colorado, Utah, and Nevada—the Far Southwest.

Just about the time the United States got this territory from Mexico some workmen discovered gold in
California. The next year thousands and thousands of
people began to flock there to hunt gold. Endless
streams of "Forty-niners" filled the trails, and many
thousands dared yellow fever and death by crossing the
Isthmus of Panama. In 1850 California came into the
Union as the thirty-first state.

WHAT THE MAP TELLS

1. Show on a map the territory which the United States
received from Mexico in the Mexican War.

2. Point out and name the states that were later made out
of this territory.

3. Show on a map the four trails to the Pacific Coast and
point out the important places along the way.

4. Looking at a map, point out the reasons why the mountains were settled before the great plains.

JUST IMAGINE

5. Imagine that you are one of the "Forty-niners" and
describe your journey over either the northern or the southern trail.

6. Imagine that you are an Indian of the Sioux tribe who
is describing to his chief the great stream of people and
wagons that he saw while with a buffalo-hunting party.

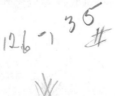

Bad roads and danger of highway robbery or attack by Indians made stagecoach travel across lonely western plains and mountains an adventure. Stagecoaches were replaced slowly by railroads and in out-of-the-way places more recently by automobiles and motor busses.

UNIT FOUR

THE TESTING OF THE NATION

Though our nation grew large and powerful and extended its boundaries from ocean to ocean, the people were not united. A quarrel arose between the North and the South over the question of slavery.

At one time there were slaves in all of the states. But the northern states passed laws freeing their slaves, while the southern people held on to theirs. Then certain men and women in the North began to say that slavery was morally wrong. They wanted Congress to do something to get rid of it. But Congress replied that it had no right to pass a law touching slavery in the states. Only the separate state governments had the right to free the slaves.

When Congress refused to pass the laws that they wanted, these earnest people in the North thought of another way to work against slavery. They said that Congress had the right to govern the territories. Therefore it had the right to pass laws forbidding anybody to take slaves into the territory west of the Mississippi River. This proposal made the southern people very angry.

The quarrel grew more and more violent after the United States got New Mexico and California, at the end of the Mexican War. The South wanted to divide the new territory and allow slavery in the southern part, but the North refused.

Some southern leaders began to say then that if their states could not get fair treatment in the Union, they must get out and form a new union in which they might manage their own government as they pleased. What could be done to save the Union?

Henry Clay, of Kentucky, and Daniel Webster, of Massachusetts, begged Congress to adopt a plan which they believed would put an end to the quarrel. This plan, called the Compromise of 1850, provided that settlers going into a territory might choose whether to have slaves or not. John C. Calhoun, of South Carolina, thought the plan would not work. He begged Congress to divide the territories equally between the North and the South. He believed that to be the only way to stop the quarrel and save the Union.

Congress followed the advice of Clay and Webster and adopted the Compromise of 1850; but Calhoun was right. It did not end the quarrel.

In 1854 the Republican party was formed. Its members were pledged to oppose slavery in the territories. In 1860 the Republicans elected Abraham Lincoln President of the United States. The southern people feared that the next step of the Republicans would be to put an end to slavery in the states. Many of them thought that the time had come to get out of the Union. Others tried to prevent the breakup of the Union.

There was a contest in each state, but those who wanted to get out of the Union won, and eleven of the southern states seceded.

The North refused to let the South go in peace. It fought to preserve the Union, and, after a war of four years, it won. The Union was saved.

STORIES FOR UNIT FOUR

Hunt, M. L., *Lucinda* (Frederick A. Stokes Company).

Page, T. N., *Two Little Confederates* (Charles Scribner's Sons).

Hill, F. T., *On the Trail of Grant and Lee* (D. Appleton-Century Company).

Hart, A. B., and Stevens, E., *Romance of the Civil War* (The Macmillan Company).

Chapter XII

THE UNION IN DANGER

Henry Clay

Mass. Hist. Society

Daniel Webster

THE NORTH AND THE SOUTH DRIFT APART

Factories in the North and plantations in the South. The people of the North and the South followed different ways of living. In the North more and more factories were built, and more and more people moved to the cities to work in them. As time went on and the factories kept on increasing, the northern people began to say that Congress ought to pass a law putting a heavy tax on goods brought from other countries. Such a tax would enable the factory owners to charge higher prices for their goods and would benefit both them and their workmen.

But most southern people lived on farms and plantations and there were few factories. They did not want

To spin and weave southern cotton into cloth many mills were
built in the North, especially in New England.

Congress to help the factories, because they did not
want to pay higher prices for the factory goods they
had to buy. So disagreement grew between the North
and the South about the tax on foreign goods.

Free workmen in the North and slaves in the South.
Another cause of disagreement grew up between the
North and the South over slavery.

The first negro slaves in the English colonies were
brought to Virginia by a Dutch ship in 1619. The
planters needed hands. There were not enough workmen in America to do all the farm work. The Indians

Cotton was put on a river boat. At the river mouth it was loaded on a seagoing ship, to be taken to northern or English cotton mills.

did not make good laborers. They liked to roam the forests and hunt. At home they liked to loaf around their wigwams, smoking and talking, while the squaws did the work. So the Virginians bought the negroes to work on their plantations.

The negroes worked well in the Virginia tobacco fields. South Carolina planters found them useful in the rice fields. Everybody wanted them. Shipowners, living mostly in the North, began to send ships to Africa and bring more and more negroes to America to sell to southern planters. Few people bought slaves in the North, because there was not much work there that the slaves could do; but there were some slaves in all the English colonies.

Soon after the Declaration of Independence all the northern states took steps to free their slaves. Many southerners, too, wished to free the slaves, but the broad cotton fields called for more and more workers, and most of the white people did not see how they could get along without slaves.

As the years passed, many northern people came to believe that slavery was wrong. They thought the government ought to do something to free the negroes. Then the South began to talk of getting out of the United States and making a new government. The southerners declared that the government had no right to free the negroes. What was to be done about this quarrel which seemed about to break up the Union?

Three great statesmen try to save the Union. As the years passed, men became more and more angry about the questions that divided the North and the South. Leading men in both parts of the country tried to find a way to end the quarrel, and we must now learn something about three of the greatest leaders.

HENRY CLAY, THE PEACEMAKER

A son of Old Virginia. Henry Clay was born in Virginia, the year after Jefferson wrote the Declaration of Independence. He was born in the same county as Patrick Henry, and, like Patrick Henry, Clay grew up to be a remarkable orator.

As a boy, Clay went to school in a log-cabin school-house and worked on a farm. When he was fifteen he got a place as office boy in a lawyer's office in Richmond and began to study law. When he was twenty years old he passed an examination and was given a license, or permit, to practice law.

Moves to Kentucky. Clay believed that he would have a better chance in the new state of Kentucky than in the old state of Virginia. So he moved to Kentucky and opened his first law office at Lexington. He was immediately successful as a lawyer, but the people gave him little time to practice law. They wanted him to help run the government, and they chose him to fill many kinds of public office.

In politics. First the people of Lexington sent him to the state legislature, where he became chairman, or speaker, of the House of Representatives. Then they sent him to Washington to be a member of Congress. You remember that he was one of the War Hawks who declared war against England in 1812.

Clay was almost constantly in government service from now on until the end of his life, more than forty years later. For a long time he was Speaker of the House of Representatives in Washington, just as he had been speaker of the legislature in Kentucky. Twice he was nominated for the presidency of the United States, but failed of election. His greatest service was in the Senate.

Playing the peacemaker. Clay loved the Union. He wanted the North and the South to live together peaceably, so that the United States could grow stronger and stronger. He believed that both North and South would become weak if anything happened to separate them.

Clay's first chance to play the peacemaker came in 1820. In that year the people in the territory of Missouri asked Congress to let Missouri come into the Union as a state. Congressmen from the North said that they would not let Missouri in unless the people would agree that no more slaves should be taken there. The South was very angry at this proposal. There were bitter arguments, and there was much hard feeling.

Finally Clay persuaded both sides to agree to an arrangement known as the Missouri Compromise. The North agreed to admit Missouri to the Union with slavery. The South agreed that no more slaves should be carried into the territories north of Missouri.

The Missouri Compromise ended the first chapter in the story of the quarrel between the North and the South over the slavery question.

Texas came into the Union in 1845 as a slave state. It is below the southern boundary line of Missouri. When the United States got the Far Southwest from Mexico, at the end of the Mexican War, the South wanted that territory to be open to slavery. But the North refused to allow slavery in any of that territory.

At once the quarrel was renewed. The South talked of withdrawing from the Union and forming a new United States of the South. Would the North allow the South to go and break up the Union? And what would the South do if the North tried to keep it from going?

Redrawn from mural in Missouri state capitol

When Missouri territory became a state, people flocked to St. Charles for the first meeting of the Missouri legislature.

Again Clay set to work to make peace. He was now an old man of seventy-two. His hair had grown white and his body feeble in the service of his beloved country. He had friends both North and South and was the most popular man in the government. If anybody could bring about a peaceable agreement, Clay could do it. He worked out a complicated set of laws known as the Compromise of 1850.

The most important part of Clay's plan was for Congress to make no rules whatever about slavery in the new territory. Let settlers go there with slaves or without them, just as they pleased. When there were enough settlers in any one part of the territory to form a state, let them decide for themselves whether they wanted it to be a slave state or a free state.

Taking all of his plan together, Clay thought that it was fair to the North and fair to the South. He worked for his plan in every way he could and with all the energy of his whole-hearted love for the Union.

DANIEL WEBSTER HELPS CLAY

Boyhood in New England. Daniel Webster was born in New Hampshire. He was five years younger than Henry Clay. As a boy he was so weak and sickly that his father did not put him to work on the farm but allowed him to roam the woods fishing and hunting. His health improved, and he grew into a strong man.

When young Daniel Webster was not roaming the woods, he was reading and studying. Like Benjamin Franklin, he read every book that he could get his hands on, and he seemed to remember everything that he read. By the time that he was fifteen he was such a brilliant student that his father determined to send him to Dartmouth College.

It was no easy thing for Ebenezer Webster to send a boy to college, for he was a poor man and had a large family to support. But he knew that it would be worth everything that he could do to give Daniel the best education possible. It is said that when he told Daniel of his plans to send him to college, the boy burst into tears, for he knew that his father could not afford the money to send him.

We may be sure that the grateful boy promised himself to make good use of his time and to repay his father by working hard. He carried out his promise. In the college town of Hanover, New Hampshire, he soon became known as an eloquent speaker. When he was only eighteen years old the people invited him to deliver the Fourth of July oration. He made a wonderful speech. Few men of any age could have equaled it.

He becomes a great lawyer. After graduating from Dartmouth, Webster taught school for a while to get money to help his brother through college. Then he turned to the study of law. He became one of the greatest lawyers that America has ever produced. It is said that his fees at one time amounted to twenty thousand dollars a year. Such a sum in that day was about the same as a hundred thousand dollars would be now. So, you see, Webster's father made no mistake when he sent his son to college.

He goes to Congress. But Webster, like Clay, had little time to practice law. In 1813 the people of New Hampshire sent him to Congress. There he met Clay and Calhoun and formed with both a friendship that lasted all the rest of his life.

After a while Webster moved to Boston. But the people of Massachusetts, too, needed a man like him in Congress and sent him back to Washington. For a long time he served in the House of Representatives. Then he was sent to the Senate.

Daniel Webster loved the Union and it distressed him to see the North and the South drifting farther and farther apart. Therefore he helped Clay's peacemaking plan. He wanted the North and South to be good friends. He did not want the Union to break up.

CALHOUN OPPOSES CLAY

Boyhood in South Carolina. John C. Calhoun was almost exactly the same age as Webster. He was born in South Carolina the year after Washington won the battle of Yorktown. His father was born in Ireland, but came to America when he was only six years old.

Calhoun's parents were well-to-do and gave him the best education that could be gotten at that time. He graduated from Yale College with all the honors of his class and then studied law.

A lifetime of government service. In 1811 the people of South Carolina sent Calhoun to Washington to represent them in Congress. There he met Clay, who became a member of Congress from Kentucky the same year. With Clay he was a War Hawk and voted to declare war against England in 1812.

Calhoun remained in Congress five years. Then President Monroe appointed him Secretary of War. He served eight years as Secretary of War. He was twice elected Vice-President. He was Secretary of State for a year. And he spent the last five years of his life in the United States Senate.

So you see these three great men together, Clay, Webster, and Calhoun. Clay was from the West, Webster from the East, and Calhoun from the very heart of the South. All of them loved the Union. All of them wanted to see the Union saved.

But in one very important thing Calhoun differed from Webster and Clay. He believed that a state had a right to get out of the Union if it wished. He stood for states' rights. Clay and Webster believed that the Union was intended to last forever and that a state could not secede or withdraw from it without the consent of all the people of the United States.

He opposes Clay's peace-making plan. Calhoun opposed Clay's plan for settling the quarrel between the North and the South. He said that slave owners should be allowed to take their slaves freely into any of the territories of the United States.

THE GREAT DEBATE IN THE SENATE

Three old men plead for the Union. These three great men spoke in the Senate at the beginning of March, 1850. Clay and Webster plead with all the power of their wonderful eloquence for the passage of Clay's plan, and Calhoun begged for fair treatment of the South.

It was one of the most solemn and important meetings that the Senate has ever held. The people of Washington crowded the Senate galleries until not even standing room was left, so anxious were they to hear the speeches.

All three of the great speakers were on the brink of the grave; they were very old men. Calhoun was too weak to deliver his speech. A friend read it for him. He tottered from the Senate after hearing it read and died three weeks later. Clay and Webster lived two years longer. But none who listened to them through those dark March days doubted that they were making their last great effort to serve the nation they had loved so well.

Clay's speech. Clay begged the Senate to agree to his plan. He said it was fair to the North and fair to the South. If the Senate did not agree to it, the southern states would try to withdraw from the Union; and that, Clay said, would mean war. For he did not believe that a state had the right to withdraw from the Union without the consent of the other states.

Webster's speech. Webster began his speech by saying that he did not wish to speak "as a Massachusetts man, nor as a northern man, but as an American." He spoke for the Union, he said, for all the people, for all parts of the country. He believed that Clay's plan was fair. He believed that it would work. And he begged the Senate to vote for it.

Calhoun's speech. Calhoun said that the plan would not work. He pointed out that the North and the South had been drifting apart for many years. They were quarreling more and more often. It seemed to him that they were quarreling nearly all the time. Even if Clay's plan were adopted, he believed that the quarrel would be sure to break out again. The only way to settle the quarrel, he said, was for Congress to divide the western territories fairly between the North and the South and let the southerners take slaves into their territories and make them slave states.

Congress agrees to Clay's plan. Congress adopted Clay's plan. The plan is known in history as the Compromise of 1850. But Calhoun was right; it did not work. The quarrel broke out again and grew more and more bitter until the North and the South came to blows and a terrible war was fought.

But all three of these great statesmen were dead before the war began. Calhoun did not see his prophecy come true; and Clay and Webster did not know that their long years of effort to prevent war had failed.

A SHORT STORY TO TELL

The ways of living in the North were different from those in the South. Many of the northern people lived in the rapidly growing cities and worked in factories. In the South most of the people lived on farms and plantations, raising cotton, tobacco, and rice. There were few factories in the southern states.

The North wanted Congress to pass laws to help the factory owners get better prices for their goods. Many northerners also wanted to free the slaves who worked the southern plantations. The South objected to both these things. The southern people did not want to pay higher prices for factory goods, nor did they want to free the slaves. So the North and the South quarreled about these two matters and about some other things as well. The South began to talk of getting out of the Union and making a United States of the South. The Union was in danger.

Henry Clay thought it would be a terrible thing to break up the Union that Washington and Madison and Hamilton and Franklin had helped to build. He worked out a plan for peace between the North and the South and begged Congress to agree to it. His plan was called the Compromise of 1850. Daniel Webster agreed with Clay, but John C. Calhoun did not believe the plan would work and opposed it. These three great men made speeches on the plan in March, 1850. Finally Congress took the advice of Clay and Webster and agreed to Clay's plan. But Calhoun was right; the Compromise of 1850 did not work.

HOW PEOPLE LIVED

1. Make two lists; one to show the way people lived and worked in the South; the other to show the way people lived and worked in the North.

GETTING THE MEANING

2. Write the answers to these questions.

What is an eloquent speaker?

Why was the settlement of the quarrel over Missouri called a compromise?

What is meant by the statement, "Webster gave a great oration before the senate"?

Calhoun said Clay's Compromise of 1850 would not work. Why was this called a prophecy?

What is meant by saying, "With the opening of the Far Southwest to settlers the slavery quarrel was renewed"?

What is a proposal? Tell about one that Clay made.

THREE GREAT MEN

3. Be able to tell the stories of the lives of Clay, Calhoun, and Webster.

4. Explain how Calhoun and Clay could both be working to help the country and yet disagree so strongly.

5. Point out the ways in which Clay, Calhoun and Webster were alike and the ways in which they were different.

2nd Semester

Chapter XIII

THE WAR BETWEEN THE NORTH AND THE SOUTH

Abraham Lincoln

Jefferson Davis

THE MISUNDERSTANDING GROWS WORSE

Clay's plan fails. Four years after Clay worked out his plan for peace, blood was shed in Kansas. The westward trails through Kansas had been leading some homeseekers to stay and settle there. One group of settlers from New England wanted to make Kansas a free state. Another group from the South wanted to make it a slave state. They quarreled and fought so fiercely that the territory was called "bleeding Kansas."

The same year (1854) some people in the North started a new political party. They called it the Republican party, and said that its main object was to keep slavery from being carried into any new territory.

The new party spread over the North like a prairie fire, but of course it had no members in the South.

If the Republican party should grow strong enough to get control of the government, it might go hard with the South. And that is exactly what happened. In 1860 the Republicans elected Abraham Lincoln President of the United States. The new party also sent many Republican members to Congress.

Abraham Lincoln on slavery. Lincoln said in one of his speeches:

" 'A house divided against itself cannot stand.' I do not expect the Union to be dissolved; I do not expect the house to fall; but I do expect that it will cease to be divided. It will become all one thing or all the other."

Lincoln believed that all the states would become slave-holding states or all would free their slaves. Remembering this speech after Lincoln was elected, many southern leaders believed that he would now work to get rid of slavery in the states. We do not know what he intended to do.

THE SOUTH WITHDRAWS FROM THE UNION

South Carolina takes the lead. The South did not wait to see what the Republican President would do. It seemed certain now that the North and the South could not live together in peace. If that was the case, said southern leaders, it was better for the South to end the quarreling by withdrawing from the Union.

The South believed that each state joined the Union by its own wish and consent. Therefore the South believed that each state could withdraw from the Union when it pleased. This was Calhoun's belief, and South Carolina, Calhoun's state, took the lead. It withdrew from the Union in December, 1860.

Other southern states follow. Six other southern states quickly followed South Carolina in declaring their connection with the Union ended. These were Mississippi, Florida, Alabama, Georgia, Louisiana, and Texas. A short time later Virginia, Arkansas, North Carolina, and Tennessee also withdrew, making eleven states in all.

The South forms a new union. In February, 1861, some men from the southern states met at Montgomery, Alabama, and formed a southern union, entirely separate from the United States. They named their union the Confederate States of America.

At first the capital of the Confederate States was at Montgomery. Later the capital was moved to Richmond, Virginia. Jefferson Davis of Mississippi became President of the Confederate States, and Alexander H. Stephens of Georgia became Vice-President.

The North refuses to let the South break up the Union. The North denied that a state had any right to secede, that is, to get out of the Union. President Lincoln said that the southern states were still in the Union, and that it was his duty to enforce the laws of the United States in the South as well as in the other states.

War between the North and the South. War between the two sections was now certain. There was no escape. The South insisted on going its own way and living its life as it pleased. The North said it should not go.

The first shot in the terrible four years' war that
followed was fired at Fort Sumter, near Charleston,
South Carolina, on April 12, 1861. President Lincoln
was trying to get food and reinforcements to the Union

Young Abraham Lincoln studying by firelight.

soldiers in Fort Sumter. The South attacked, fired the
first shot, and captured the fort before the new Union
soldiers arrived.

NORTHERN AND SOUTHERN LEADERS

President Lincoln. Abraham Lincoln, the head of the
Union government and commander in chief of the
army and navy, was a tall, good humored man with

much of the appearance and a good many of the ways of a backwoodsman. In fact, he was born in the backwoods of Kentucky on February 12, 1809. His father was always an easy-going pioneer. Young Abraham grew up in a log cabin with a leaky roof, in the midst of a small clearing that barely raised food enough for the family.

When the boy was seven years old, his father moved to Indiana. But the Lincoln family remained as poor in Indiana as it had been in Kentucky until Abraham was strong enough to take on his own shoulders the work of the farm. Then the Lincolns got along a little better, for Abraham was a tireless worker.

Lincoln had but six months of schooling in his whole life. But he read over and over again the few books that he could borrow, and he thought about what he read. As a boy he studied Webster's spelling book, a life of Washington, Franklin's life of himself, and a small history of the United States. He read *Robinson Crusoe, Aesop's Fables,* and the *Arabian Nights.* As he grew older, he read the Bible and Henry Clay's speeches. He was a grown man before he studied grammar.

He taught himself to speak and write clear, simple English by constant practice. When he read or heard a statement that did not seem to him as clear and simple as it ought to be, he tried to express it in his own words so plainly that any boy he knew could understand it.

This practice grew into a habit with him, and when he was a middle-aged man he said of himself, "I am never easy now when I am handling a thought, till I have bounded it north, bounded it south, bounded it east, and bounded it west." He tried to be able to say what he had to say in such a way that the people who were listening to him would understand exactly what he meant.

When Lincoln was twenty-one his father moved again, this time to Illinois. Lincoln went with him, built him a comfortable cabin, split rails and fenced a farm, and then left home. He went to Springfield, studied law, and was soon practicing law. His skill in telling funny stories made him a favorite among the lawyers who gathered at the courthouse on court days. And his simple, kindly manners made him popular with juries, and with people who had him to look after their law business. He was successful.

Like most lawyers of that day, Lincoln was interested in politics. In 1834 he was elected to the Illinois legislature. In 1846 he was a member of Congress. He belonged to the Whig party, the party of Henry Clay. In 1858 he was a member of the new Republican party, and ran against his old friend, Stephen A. Douglas, for the United States Senate. Douglas defeated him, but the speeches that Lincoln made during this campaign turned the eyes of the whole nation upon him. From that time he was a marked man, and when the time came to choose presidential candidates for the election of 1860, the Republicans picked him to lead the party.

Lincoln was a man of great mind and great heart. Remembering the hardships of his own early life, he sympathized with all poor and unfortunate people. He sympathized with the slaves, but he also saw some of the troubles that the southern people saw in the way of freeing the slaves. He knew that the slavery question had more than one side.

We do not know what Lincoln would have done about slavery if the eleven southern states had not withdrawn from the Union. He said many times that slavery in the states was a matter that the states alone had the right to control for themselves; and that Congress had no right to interfere in affairs of the states.

At the same time, he believed that a state had no right to withdraw from the Union; and, as President, he believed that it was his duty to preserve the Union.

Jefferson Davis. The President of the Confederate States was nine months older than Lincoln. Like Lincoln, he was born in Kentucky. Lincoln's father moved northward to Indiana, and remained as poor and easy-going as he had been in Kentucky. Davis's father moved southward to the Mississippi Territory, and grew wealthy raising cotton.

The two boys therefore grew up in very different ways. Young Davis had the best of schooling and entered Transylvania University at Lexington, Kentucky, at the age of thirteen. From there he went to West Point, and was trained to be a military officer.

After graduating from West Point, Davis remained in the army until 1835, when he resigned. He returned to the army in 1846 to command a regiment in the Mexican War. He made a name for himself in the battles in northern Mexico, but his fame is due to his political life and not to his service in the army.

When the fighting in northern Mexico was over he returned to Mississippi and was sent by the state to the United States Senate. Then for four years he was Secretary of War, and again a member of the Senate.

President Lincoln's first call for volunteers was for three months' service. The war lasted four years.

Jefferson Davis probably had more power and influence than any other man in Washington from 1853 to 1861. Both President Pierce and President Buchanan used to ask his advice about important matters of government, and they usually did what he advised.

Davis did not want the South to leave the Union. Like Henry Clay, he believed the rights of the South

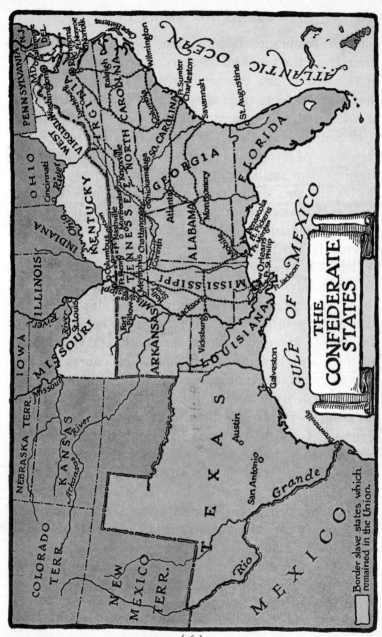

THE CONFEDERATE STATES

Border slave states which remained in the Union.

could be made safe in the Union. When his state withdrew from the Union, however, he sadly took his leave
of the Senate and returned to his Mississippi plantation. It was from there that he was called to head the
new Confederate government.

President Davis, like President Lincoln, was a tall,
thin man, of irregular features. He was a man of great
dignity. But unlike Lincoln, he could not tell funny
stories and mix easily with everyday people. For this
and other reasons he did not arouse the warm affection
that many people felt for Lincoln. But people respected Jefferson Davis, and sometimes feared him.

Ulysses S. Grant. The greatest general on the Union
side was Ulysses S. Grant. He was born in Ohio in
1822. When he was seventeen years old, his father got
him an appointment to West Point, to be trained for
the army. He did not like the work at West Point,
but he compelled himself to finish the course. When
he was graduated he became a lieutenant in the army.

His first important military service was in the
Mexican War. He fought throughout the war, under
General Taylor in the North and under General
Scott in the South. At the end of the war he was
promoted for bravery and efficiency to the rank of cap-
tain.

After the Mexican War Grant resigned from the
army and went into business. He had not liked the
army work, but he did not like business either. He
turned from one thing to another, storekeeping, farming, lumbering, hauling wood. Finally he was reduced
to doing odd jobs that barely enabled him to keep body

and soul together. Sometimes he had hardly enough money to buy food.

When the great war between the North and the South began he was thirty-nine years old, and seemed to be a total failure. He was shabby, discouraged, and without money. After some difficulty and delay, he obtained a command as colonel of an Illinois regiment.

At last he seems to have liked his work. He proved himself a great commander. In 1863 President Lincoln made him commander in chief of all the Union forces.

The following year the President moved Grant to Virginia and gave him the task of crushing General Lee and breaking down the Confederacy. This task Grant finished in April, 1865, and brought the war to an end.

General Grant did not look like a great general. He was a short, heavily built man, with reddish brown hair and beard, and he liked to wear an old, shabby uniform.

After the war General Grant was twice elected President of the United States, and served two terms, from 1869 to 1877.

Robert E. Lee. The greatest southern general was Robert Edward Lee. He was born in Virginia, on January 19, 1807, and was therefore a little older than Lincoln and Jefferson Davis.

A northern historian, James Ford Rhodes, has described Lee as he was at the beginning of the war. He says: "Lee was now fifty-four years old. His face showed the ruddy glow of health and his head was without a gray hair. He was physically and morally a

General Grant, under fire, planning his campaign.

splendid example of manhood. He had the best blood of Virginia in his veins. He was honest, sincere, simple, kindhearted, patient, refined, and courteous. Dignified and proud, never lacking self-command, he was in every respect a true man."

No doubt Lee got his liking for military life from his father, Henry Lee, who was one of Washington's most trusted officers. Henry Lee was called "Light-Horse Harry" on account of his dashing cavalry charges.

Lee's life was very different from the lives of Lincoln and Grant. During all of his childhood he was taught by private tutors, and studied hard. At the age of eighteen he was appointed to West Point. General Andrew Jackson got him the appointment. At West Point he still studied hard, and finished second in his class of forty-six, without a single demerit or black mark against his record. Duty, he said, was the greatest word in the English language, and throughout his whole life he did his duty as he saw it.

For thirty-two years, from 1829 until 1861, Lee was always in the service of the United States government. General Scott said that he was the most useful officer in the Mexican War and declared that he would, if

A train of supply wagons of the Confederate army on the march,

given a chance, prove himself to be the greatest general
of his time.

At the beginning of the war between the North and
the South, Lee was offered the command of the Union
army, but he did not accept. He said that he could
think of no misfortune more terrible than the breaking
up of the Union, but that he could "take no part in an
invasion of the southern states." He could not lead
an army against the people of his own state. The wisdom of the first view expressed, and the home-love of
the second tell us much about the man.

So, when Virginia withdrew from the Union, Lee
resigned his place in the United States army and took
command of the Virginia soldiers. From this position
he was promoted to be commander in chief of all the
Confederate armies in northern Virginia. It was his
duty to defend Richmond and the Confederate government from the Union armies.

For nearly three years General Lee withstood northern attack. He proved himself, as Scott had said he
would, one of the greatest commanders of the day.
Soldiers of all nations have studied General Lee's campaigns and have declared them models of military skill.

But month after month Lee's army grew smaller. He
could not fight without losing men, and the South could
not make up his losses. It was worn out. Finally on
April 9, 1865, Lee surrendered to General Grant all
that was left of his shattered, starving army, and the
war was over.

General Lee then became president of Washington
and Lee University, at Lexington, Virginia.

HOW THE WAR WAS CARRIED ON

The work of the northern navy. The North used the navy to guard and blockade the southern coast, so that the South could neither sell its cotton and sugar and tobacco in Europe nor buy clothing and war supplies for its army.

At first the South had no warships, and the northern navy was entirely successful. It closed the southern harbors, sailed up and down the coast, and prevented the South from carrying on foreign trade.

As the South had few factories, the blockade was a terrible hardship for the people. Most of the negroes remained at home and continued to work the plantations, so that food was plentiful enough. But factory goods became scarcer and scarcer. Tools wore out and could not be replaced. The railroads, engines, and cars broke down and could not be repaired.

The southern government built furnaces and iron foundries and powder mills to make guns, cannon, and ammunition; but they could not supply the needs of the southern soldiers. To clothe the soldiers, spinning wheels and looms were set up in every home, and women and girls spun and wove and knitted from morning till night.

Medicines gave out and no more could be had, except what could be smuggled in through Mexico. Coffee gave out, but the southern people found that parched corn and okra seed made a good drink. Soda gave out, and the ashes of burnt corn cobs were used to make the cornbread rise. These and many other things had to be used by the southern people to take the place of things that the northern warships kept them from buying.

In the North all was different. There the factories worked overtime, turning out cannon and munitions, uniforms, wagons, railroad rails, engines, and cars. And everything that they could not make, they could buy. For all the world was open to the North, and all nations were ready to sell it what it needed. They were just as ready to sell to the South, but the North had shut the door. Foreign goods could not get in.

Just imagine that a wall were built around your county or town so that nothing could be shipped in or out, and you will get a very good idea of the success of the northern blockade. The Northern ships were like a wall built around the South. Goods could not get through.

The North had more men than the South. When the war began, the North had twenty-two million people. The South had five million white people and four million negroes. During all the four years of the war, European immigrants entered the North to work in the factories and on the farms, but very few went to the South.

The South won many battles, but became constantly weaker. When it lost a man it could not replace him, but the North had a man to put in the place of every one that it lost.

General Grant comes to the front. The first important success of the Union army in the West was the capture (1862) of Fort Donelson in Tennessee, near the mouth of the Tennessee River. General Grant commanded the Union army there, and his victories won him fame and promotion.

Grant captures Vicksburg. We cannot tell in this book the story of the desperate fighting that followed. Resisting bravely, the Confederate soldiers fell back, and General Grant advanced southward. Through Tennessee and Mississippi toward Vicksburg he marched. If he could take Vicksburg he could control the whole Mississippi River. The South would be split in two, for the navy had already captured New Orleans. Vicksburg surrendered on July 4, 1863.

Arkansas, northern Louisiana, and Texas remained free of Union troops, but they were now cut off from the rest of the Confederate states.

Grant forces the Confederate armies from Tennessee. Grant turned next to eastern Tennessee, and fought some terrible battles around Chattanooga, which drove the Confederate armies southward toward Georgia. In 1864 President Lincoln moved Grant to Virginia to oppose General Lee. General William T. Sherman took Grant's place in the Georgia campaign.

Sherman's march to the sea. Sherman formed the plan of capturing Atlanta and then marching through the heart of Georgia to Savannah. He believed that in this way he could hasten the end of the war.

Sherman began his march in November, 1864, and captured Savannah a few days before Christmas. Wherever he went his army took horses, mules, cattle, hogs, chickens, and every living thing. He blew up bridges, tore up railroads, burned the ties, and twisted and bent the rails around trees, so that they could never be used again.   He was trying in every way to make it impossible for the southern people to keep up the war much longer.

General Sherman believed that he destroyed southern property worth a hundred million dollars. Besides the terrible loss to the people of Georgia, the destruction of the railroad cut off the supplies that General Lee's army had been getting from Georgia. Very soon his men were almost starving.

The march to the sea cut the Confederate States into two widely separated halves. Virginia and the Carolinas were in the East and Arkansas and Texas in the West. The Union army held the territory between these two halves.

The northern army in Virginia. The task of the Union army in Virginia was to capture Richmond and the Confederate government.   But Lee commanded the southern army in Virginia, and month after month and year after year he held the Union forces at bay. They could not break through. They could not get to Richmond.

All the time, however, the South was using up men, horses were being killed, wagons were destroyed, engines and cars were wearing out on the railroads. It became harder and harder to get men to fill the places of those killed and wounded in battle. And it became harder and harder to get the food and other supplies that an army must always have.

When Grant was moved to Virginia, he could afford to lose two or three men for every one that Lee lost, and still remain the stronger. Therefore he determined to fight and fight. If necessary, he would fight until all Lee's men were gone. His losses were terrible, but he was resolved not to stop. He said he would capture Richmond and break up the Confederate government no matter what the cost.

Lee surrenders. Finally the time came when Lee had scarcely one man to Grant's four. Some of Lee's men were barefooted. All of them were hungry. He could get no more men; he could get no more food; and Grant's army was all around him.

The end had come. General Lee's army could fight no longer.

On April 9, 1865, General Lee sent General Grant a note, asking for a meeting to discuss terms for the surrender of all that was left of his army.

Twenty years later General Grant wrote an account of the meeting in words that proved him to be a kind and generous man as well as a great general. He said:

"What General Lee's feelings were I do not know. As he was a man of much dignity, and controlled the expression of his face, it was impossible to say whether he felt glad that the end had finally come, or felt sad because the South had lost, and was too manly to show it.

"Whatever his feelings, they were entirely hidden from me. But my own feelings, which had been jubilant on the receipt of his letter, were sad and depressed. I felt like anything rather than rejoicing at the downfall of a foe who had fought so long and so bravely and had suffered so much.

General Lee's farewell to his soldiers.

"We soon fell into a conversation about old army times. Our talk grew so pleasant that I almost forgot the object of our meeting. After the talk had run in this style for some time, General Lee called my attention to the object of our meeting."

General Lee asked General Grant to write out the terms for the surrender of the southern army. Grant then wrote out a very short statement: All cannon, guns, wagons, and other property belonging to the Confederate government were to be turned over to the Union general.

Lee's officers and men were to keep their horses and

personal property and go to their homes, after giving their word that they would not again fight against the United States.

General Lee thanked General Grant for allowing his men to keep their horses, for they would need them now to work their farms.

As Lee rode sadly back to his men, they gathered around him, weeping and wringing his hand. Tears came to his eyes, and in a choking voice he said: "We have fought through the war together. I have done the best I could for you. My heart is too full to say more."

The next day he issued a farewell address, thanking the men for their faithful service, and advising them to go home and obey the laws.

PRESIDENT LINCOLN'S PLAN FOR THE SOUTH

President Lincoln frees the slaves. During the war President Lincoln issued a proclamation declaring slavery at an end in the Confederate states. Now his plan was to bring the South back into the Union after getting the southern people to agree to free the slaves.

The death of Lincoln. Most of the southern people were ready to accept President Lincoln's plan; but the plan was changed by a tragic accident. On April 14, President Lincoln was shot and killed by an insane actor while he was at the theatre in Washington. This mad act took the President's wise leadership from Congress, and Congress now refused to carry out his plan. But for that murder the South would probably have been spared much sorrow and our history a great blot.

CONGRESS PUNISHES THE SOUTH

Hardships of the South. Andrew Johnson, the Vice-President who now took Lincoln's place, was from Tennessee. He was a southern man. He wanted to carry out Lincoln's plan. He was a good man, but he was not so wise as Lincoln had been. He did not know how to get along with other men. He quarreled with Congress, and after a while Congress simply took the government out of his hands.

Congress believed that the South ought to be punished. Therefore it took away from many of the southern white men the right to vote and hold office, and gave the right to vote to negroes, who were now free.

Mean and dishonest white men flocked into the South from the North. They put themselves at the head of the negroes, took charge of the state governments, plundered and injured the South without mercy.

Leaders in Congress feared that southerners would again enslave the negroes, so they put soldiers into the South to protect them, and also to protect the new state governments.

The Southern people regain control of their states. For ten years the condition in the South was very unhappy. But gradually southern white men again got control of their states and put out the dishonest office holders.

At the same time people in the North changed their minds. They began to say that the South had been punished enough, that the people ought to be allowed to govern themselves.

President Hayes removed the soldiers from the

South, and by the end of 1877 the southern states were again under the control of their own people.

The hard years from the time the war ended until the southern people again got control of their state governments are called the Period of Reconstruction. It was supposed to be a time for recovering from the losses and suffering caused by the war. But the real reconstruction came much later.

A SHORT STORY TO TELL

The Compromise of 1850 did not work, so the quarrel between the North and the South began again. Many of the southern people wanted slavery allowed in all the country. People in the North started a new political party, the Republican party, to oppose this. In 1860 they elected Abraham Lincoln President.

We do not know what Lincoln would have done about slavery, but the southern States did not wait to see. They withdrew from the old Union and formed a new union of the South, which they called the Confederate States of America.

President Lincoln believed that a state did not have a right to get out of the Union. He called for soldiers to keep the southern states from withdrawing. President Jefferson Davis likewise called for troops to defend the Confederate States, and a terrible war began.

The North was very much stronger than the South. It had more men, more ships, more money, and more factories than the South, and it won.

During the war President Lincoln set the slaves free. He was a kind man, and he wanted to make it easy for

the southern states to come back into the Union when
the war was over, but he was killed just as the war
ended. The leaders of Congress had laws passed which
placed parts of the South under military rule for ten
years.

TELL WHY

1. there were no Republicans in the South.
2. the southern states left the Union.
3. Grant was better able to keep on fighting than was Lee.
4. the Period of Reconstruction was a hard time for the
South.
5. the North was so successful on the sea.
6. the South finally surrendered to the North.

WORDS TO USE

7. Use these words in sentences that will tell about the
War between the North and the South.

reinforcements   smuggled
preserve   munitions
blockade   proclamation
resigned   Reconstruction

MAP STUDY

8. Study the map on page 177. Explain how Grant and
Sherman divided the Confederate States. What effect did
this have on the South?

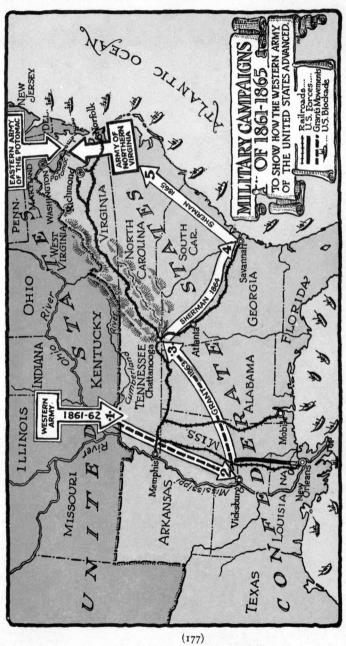

This map shows the North's plan of attack. The North's eastern army never broke through the South's defense until Grant took command. While the western army was moving to Vicksburg, down to the eastern coast and then towards Richmond, the northern navy tightened the blockade of southern ports.

UNIT FIVE

THE CONQUEST OF MOUNTAINS AND PLAINS

The last large section of our country to be occupied by white people seeking homes was the region of the high plains and the Rocky Mountains. If you want to know why this was so, you can find the answer in your geography.

This was the region of famous trails—the trail to Oregon and California, the Santa Fé Trail, and the trail of the Southern Overland Mail. It was the region of the Pony Express, the home of the fierce plains Indians, and of countless herds of buffalo.

Gold seekers led the way to the settlement of the region. Rich gold deposits were discovered in various parts of the west, and miners flocked to the mines. Towns and mining camps sprang up in the states that we now call Colorado, Nevada, Idaho, Montana, and South Dakota. Along with the miners went merchants, inn-keepers, and an occasional farmer.

Gradually the white people began to learn about many parts of the West. Ranchmen and farmers followed the lead of the miners and began to settle the plains. Driving herds of long-horned cattle up from Texas, the ranchmen fattened them on the northern plains and shipped them to Chicago, where they were sold for beef.

The ranchmen did not welcome the farmers, because they wanted all of the land for themselves. The cowboys would cut the wire fences of the farms and let the cattle destroy the crops. They would try to frighten the "nesters" away. But the "nester" had come to stay. The government gave him a homestead. He fenced it with barbed wire, drilled wells to get water, set up windmills, and learned a new method of farming called dry-land farming.

Finally the ranchmen and farmers learned to live together peaceably. Then the country became prosperous. Cities and towns grew up. Railroads were built. And schools and churches were established.

The coming of the white people was hard on the Indians. They wanted to continue their wild life, roaming over the plains and living on the buffaloes. But the white people killed the buffaloes and fenced the plains. What could the poor Indians do?

The government tried to put the Indians on reservations, where they could be fed and clothed and taught the ways of the white men. But they did not want to learn the white man's ways. They made war on the whites and tried to drive them away. The government sent soldiers to protect the settlers, and the Indians were finally subdued.

STORIES OF INTEREST FOR UNIT FIVE

Wilder, Mrs. L. I., *Little House on the Prairie* (Harper Brothers).

James, Will, *In the Saddle With Uncle Bill* (Charles Scribner's Sons).

Fogler, D., and Nicol, N., *Rusty Pete of the Lazy Ab* (The Macmillan Company).

Driggs, H. R., *The Pony Express Goes Through* (Frederick A. Stokes Company).

Carr, M. J., *Children of the Covered Wagon* (Thomas Y. Crowell Company).

Chapter XIV

THE OPENING OF MOUNTAINS
AND PLAINS

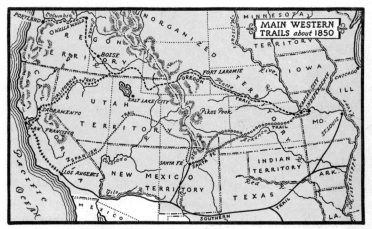

A half century of history is linked with these trails.

THE EMIGRANT TRAILS

A lesson in geography. We must turn now to the story
of some of the states that came into the Union after the
War between the North and the South.

In Chapter IX we followed the march of the pioneers to Oregon. In Chapter XI we saw how the
United States got California, and how the great gold
rush of 1849 carried many thousands of people to
the Pacific coast in a single year. Though the rush
slowed down after the first year, nearly half a million

people had crossed the continent to California, Oregon, and Washington by 1861, when the war began. But most of the land between these far western settlements and the Mississippi River remained unsettled. If you wish to know the reason why, you must turn to your geography.

Most of the land west of the Mississippi River is made up of high, dry plains and lofty mountains. The first emigrants were accustomed to a country where heavy rains fall and where timber was convenient to build houses and fences. They did not know how to live on the plains, where the rains seldom fall and where few trees grow except on the banks of the streams and along the slopes of the mountains. So the emigrants passed on to California and Oregon and Washington.

The trails to the west. There were three great trails to the West. The oldest was the Santa Fé Trail. It started at Independence, on the Missouri River, and crossed the present states of Kansas, Oklahoma, and New Mexico to Santa Fé. Later it was extended across Arizona into southern California.

The Southern Overland Trail had two starting points, one point at St. Louis, Missouri, and the other at Memphis, Tennessee. The trails from St. Louis and Memphis came together in Arkansas. Then the main trail crossed Texas, New Mexico, and Arizona to southern California.

The third and most famous trail was the Oregon-California Trail. It started from various points on the Missouri River—from Independence, St. Joseph, and Atchison. It crossed Kansas, Nebraska, a little corner of Colorado, and Wyoming to Utah. At Fort Bridger, near the Great Salt Lake, it forked. One branch turned northward across Idaho and went on to Oregon and Washington. The other branch turned southward and, after crossing Utah and Nevada, led to Sacramento and San Francisco in California. From the main trail other trails branched north and south to the Dakotas, Montana, and Colorado.

Wherever it was possible, the trail followed the course of a stream, but sometimes there were long marches across the desert where men and animals suffered terribly and sometimes died of thirst. Here the trail was marked by abandoned wagons and the bleached bones of the unfortunate animals that had dragged them so far.

THE OVERLAND MAIL

Carrying the mail by sea. In 1849, the very first year of the gold rush, the government arranged to send mail to Oregon and California by sea. Ships took the mail to Colon, on the Isthmus of Panama. There it was transferred to pack mules and carried across the Isthmus to the city of Panama. Then another ship took it on board and carried it to San Francisco.

It sometimes took six or seven weeks to get a letter to California by this route. As more people moved to the West they wanted faster and safer service.

The Southern Overland Mail. In 1857 the postmaster general let it be known that the government wanted to start an overland mail service to California. The plan was to have stages traveling both ways all the time.

A group of men headed by John Butterfield of New York made a contract with the government to carry the mail. Twice a week a coach left St. Louis and traveled day and night until it arrived at San Francisco, nearly three thousand miles away. At the same time other coaches started from San Francisco and traveled night and day until they reached St. Louis. Traveling in this way and stopping only long enough to change horses and let the passengers get a hasty lunch at the stations, the coaches made the trip in twenty-four or twenty-five days. The coaches went by the southern route, passing through Arkansas, Oklahoma, Texas, New Mexico, and Arizona before getting to California.

Hardships and dangers of the trip. Passengers on the "Overland" suffered many hardships and some dangers. The coaches were usually crowded and there was no room for a passenger to stretch himself out and take a nap. He had to sleep sitting up. In some places the road was so rough that the coach was in constant danger of turning over, and often it did turn over. There were no bridges and there was always difficulty in crossing streams. The Indians rarely attacked the coaches, but they often stole the horses and mules at the stations and delayed the trip by preventing the drivers from getting fresh animals for the next stage of the journey.

The end of the Southern Overland Mail. When the war began between the North and the South, the government quit sending the mail over the southern trail. The Butterfield Company moved its horses and coaches to Kansas and began to carry the mail to California by way of Denver and Salt Lake City.

Moving freight to the far west

FREIGHTING ACROSS THE PLAINS

The settlement of Colorado and Utah. When the war began between the North and the South there were nearly a hundred thousand people in the mountains and plains west of Kansas. Most of these were in Colorado and Utah.

The members of the Mormon church in Utah were farmers and cattle raisers. They raised their own food and made their own clothing, so that they did not need to buy much from the stores in Missouri and Kansas.

But nearly all of the people in Colorado and Wyoming were miners. They spent their time searching for gold and had to buy nearly everything that they used. They needed food and clothing and boots and blankets. They needed tobacco and soap, powder and lead, picks and shovels, and dozens of other things that must be brought from the towns on the Missouri River, a thousand miles away.

Then there were the soldiers in scattered forts throughout the West. They, too, must have regular supplies of food and clothing and ammunition.

How could these things be gotten to the people who needed them? There were no railroads as there are now. The mail coaches were too small to carry much freight, and there were too few of them. The only way to get goods to the West was to take them on packhorses or in wagons. Since one wagon could carry more goods than twenty horses, most of the freight was hauled across the plains in wagons.

The freight trains on the plains. The firm of Russell, Majors, and Waddell did most of the hauling. One year they sent thirty-five hundred wagons across the plains. Each wagon was loaded with five or six thousand pounds of freight and was drawn by twelve oxen, yoked together in pairs. The wagons traveled in groups of twenty-five. These groups were called trains. Sometimes, when there was danger from the Indians, the drivers kept the wagons close together, but when there was no danger the train was stretched out two or three miles long.

An adventure with Indians. Mr. Majors, who was once traveling with a small train of ten wagons and a hundred and thirty oxen, had a thrilling adventure with Indian thieves. This is the way he told the story in a very interesting book that he wrote a long time ago:

"Arriving one evening at a stream called One Hundred and Ten, I camped for the night. I unyoked my oxen and turned them upon the grass. Finding the grass so good and the animals so weary with the day's work, I thought they would not stroll away, and therefore did not put out any guard as was my custom.

"At early dawn on the following morning I arose, saddled my horse, and told my assistant to arouse the teamsters, so they could be ready to yoke their teams as soon as I drove them into the corral, which was formed by the wagons. In rounding them up before reaching the wagons, I discovered that some were missing. I then made a circle looking for the trail of the missing oxen, which I soon found.

"I had not traveled more than a mile when I discovered the tracks of Indian ponies. I then knew the Indians had driven off my oxen. I was unarmed, having left my gun at the camp, but I expected to overtake them at any moment and did not return for it. So on and on I went, galloping my horse most of the time, until I had gone about twelve miles from my camp. I passed through a skirt of timber that divided one portion of the open prairie from the other, and there overtook thirty-four head of my oxen resting from their travel.

"About sixty yards to the east of the cattle were six painted Indian braves, who had dismounted from their horses. Each one was leaning against his horse, with his right hand resting upon the saddle and his left holding his gun. I came upon them suddenly. The timber prevented them from seeing me until I was within a few yards of them.

Indians often watched the emigrant trails for a chance to steal horses or oxen.

"I threw up my hand, went in a lope around my oxen, giving some yells, and told them they could go back to the wagons on the trail they had come. They at once heeded me and started. I never saw six meaner or more surprised looking men than those six braves were. I think they thought I had an armed party just behind me.

"So I followed my cattle, and left the six savages standing in dismay. We were soon out of sight in the forest, and that was the last that I saw of the six braves who had been sent out by their chief the night before to steal the oxen.

"But I was not to get off so easily. When I was about half-way back to the wagons I looked ahead and saw a large body of Indians coming toward me. They proved to be under the command of their chief and were armed. They raised a hideous yell and started toward me at the top of their horses' speed. If my oxen had not been driven so far and become tired, I should have had a wild stampede. But the animals only ran a few hundred yards before I succeeded in stopping them.

"By this time the Indians had reached me and my cattle. The braves surrounded the cattle, and the chief came at the top of his horse's speed directly toward me. He had his gun drawn up to strike me with it. Of course I did not allow him to get in striking distance. I turned my horse and put spurs to him. He was a splendid animal, and it was easy for me to keep out of the reach of the vicious chief. He did not want to kill me but desired to scare me so that they could take the oxen.

"The chief chased me off three times, but I always followed him back nearly to the cattle. The third time that I returned the chief and one of the warriors armed with a bow and arrow were sitting on their horses close to the oxen. They dashed toward me and the brave tried to grab my bridle. If he had caught it, he would have thrown me off my horse and then the Indians would have gotten away with both the horse and the oxen, leaving me to walk back to the wagons. But I was too quick for him and got away.

"Again I reined up my horse and again the two

Indians came toward me. When they were about thirty feet away the brave suddenly drew his bow at full bend, with a sharp pointed steel in the end of the arrow. He aimed at my heart and I felt a severe pain at the spot where the arrow would have struck me had he shot. But he did not shoot. With his arrow pointed, he shouted as loud as he could, 'Say!'

"I did not know what he meant, but the chief held up ten fingers and pointed at the cattle. Then I understood that he was asking for ten oxen. I felt that I could not spare that number and go on with my train, so I refused. He then threw up five fingers. Again I shook my head. He then motioned me to say how many I would give, and I held up one finger. The moment I did so he gave the word of command to his braves, who were still dancing and screaming round the cattle. They whirled into line, selected one of the animals so quickly that one had hardly time to think, and left thirty-three of the oxen and myself standing in the prairie.

"I think they were afraid some of my party would overtake me. There was no danger of that, had they only known it, for on my return I found all my men at the wagons wondering what had become of me. I had left the camp at daylight and it was after noon when I returned."*

THE PONY EXPRESS

The beginning of the Pony Express. The Southern Overland Mail took letters from St. Louis to San Fran-

---

*Slightly adapted from Alexander Majors' *Seventy Years on the Frontier* (Rand, McNally and Company, 1893).

cisco in twenty-four or twenty-five days, but that was not quick enough for the Californians. So Senator Gwin, one of California's two representatives in the United States Senate at Washington, made an arrangement for California to get quicker service. He talked the matter over with Russell, Majors, and Waddell. They were the men who were already doing the great freighting business across the plains, and they agreed to put on a pony express to carry only important mail.

A great deal of work had to be done before the pony express could be started. First, it was necessary to build camps, or stations, every twelve or fifteen miles. These camps consisted of pens for the horses and cabins for the men who took care of them. There were a hundred and ninety stations between St. Joseph, Missouri, and Sacramento, California, the two ends of the line.

Then it was necessary to buy five hundred strong, swift horses and distribute them along the line so that there would always be two or three at each station.

Finally there was the most important matter of all, the employment of the riders. There must be eighty of these, strong and wiry and brave, but the smaller they were the better, because large men would tire the horses and slow them down. Most of the riders weighed less than a hundred and thirty-five pounds.

The Pony Express on the trail. The first mail by the Pony Express was delivered in April, 1860. Every day a rider set out from St. Joseph, Missouri, and another from Sacramento, California. Each carried ten pounds of letters, written on the thinnest of tissue paper. The charge for each letter was five dollars in gold.

Day and night, rain or shine, in sand storm or snow, the riders urged their tough little ponies to the top of their speed. At each station they changed horses, gulped down a drink of water or a cup of coffee, and dashed away. Some riders had a run of sixty-five miles. Some rode more than a hundred miles. One day they rode east and the next day they rode west. At the end of each run another rider received the little bag of precious letters and carried it on.

Dangers and hardships of the riders. The Pony Express riders had no easy time. Sometimes they were chased by Indians and sometimes by bandits. Often a tired rider dashed into a station only to find no one there to carry the mail forward. In such cases there was only one thing to do. He must go on until he met the next rider, perhaps a hundred miles away. Then, without resting, he might have to start back to his home station, carrying the mail that he got from the rider that he met. Whatever happened, the mail must go on. For all this danger and hard work the riders were paid a hundred and twenty-five dollars a month.

Buffalo Bill as a Pony Express rider. Probably the most famous of all the Pony Express riders was a slender, dark-haired boy of sixteen named William F. Cody. We shall learn later how he got the name of "Buffalo Bill." In the story of his life which he wrote he tells about his experiences and adventures. He says:

"Mr. Slade assigned me to duty on the road from Red Buttes, on the North Platte, to the Three Crossings of the Sweetwater—a distance of Seventy-six miles— and I began riding at once.

It is not a great many years, but it is a long way in the history of mail carrying, from the Pony Express rider to the mail plane.

"One day when I galloped into Three Crossings, my home station, I found that the rider who was expected to take the trip out on my arrival had gotten into a drunken row the night before and been killed. This left the division without a rider and the superintendent asked me to make the trip until another rider was secured.

"The distance to the next station, Rocky Ridge, was eighty-five miles, through a very bad and dangerous country, but I agreed to try it. I started promptly from Three Crossings without more than a moment's rest and pushed on. I made the round trip of three hundred and twenty-two miles back to Red Buttes without a

single mishap and on time. This was the longest Pony
Express journey ever made.

"A week after making this trip I was jumped by a
band of Sioux Indians, who dashed out from a sand
ravine nine miles west of Horse Creek. They were
armed with pistols and gave me a close call with several
bullets, but it fortunately happened that I was mounted
on the fleetest horse belonging to the Express Company.
Being cut off from retreat back to Horseshoe, I put
spurs to my horse, and lying flat on his back, kept
straight on for Sweetwater, the next station, which I
reached without accident, my pursuers left behind.

"At Sweetwater, however, I found a sorry condition
of affairs, as the Indians had made a raid on the station
the morning of my adventure with them, and, after
killing the stocktender, they had driven off all the
horses, so that I was unable to get a remount. I therefore continued on to the next station, twelve miles
farther. Thus I made a run of twenty-four miles with
one horse.

"During the winter of 1860 and the spring of 1861
I remained at Horseshoe, occasionally riding Pony Express and taking care of stock. But I met with no
further adventure worthy to be recorded."*

The end of the Pony Express. The Pony Express cut
down the time of the trip from the Missouri River to
California to ten days. The distance was nearly two
thousand miles, so that the horses and riders had to
travel two hundred miles every twenty-four hours.

---

*Adapted slightly from Buffalo Bill, *Story of the Wild West* (Copyright
by H. S. Smith, 1888).

The Pony Express came to an end after running about two years. The telegraph wires were extended to California and the fast mail was no longer necessary.

We must now take up the story of the building of the railroads across the continent. The railroads put an end to the long hauls of the ox-trains and the stage coaches.

THE STORY OF THE RAILROADS

Small beginnings. As late as 1860, when Lincoln was elected President, there were very few railroads, and the main lines were not as good as sidetracks are now. The iron rails were light, and quickly wore out. The engines were small, and burned wood for fuel. They puffed showers of sparks and burning chips from their enormous smokestacks, but with all their puffing they could pull no more than ten or twelve loaded cars. The cars, too, were small. The passenger cars were hardly larger than our trolley cars.

Ox-wagon, stagecoach, and Pony Express. Most of the hauling of freight in 1860, when Lincoln was elected, was done by wagons drawn by horses, mules, and oxen. Much of the traveling was still done on horseback and in stagecoaches. There were only a few miles of railroad west of the Mississippi River.

The day of great things. But we no longer travel and send our mail as our grandfathers did. Now our hundred and thirty million people have more than two hundred and forty thousand miles of railroad in their country. Placed end to end, the steel track roads would go ten times around the earth. Great engines, burning coal or oil for fuel, pull twenty times the

Travel by stagecoach was slow, uncomfortable, and apt to be
interrupted by delays. Compare this with our trains which travel
at great speed while the passengers ride in comfort.

amount of freight that the busy, puffing little engines
used to haul. Cars today are built of steel, and the
passenger cars are like palaces on wheels. They are
large and comfortable, air conditioned, furnished with
easy chairs, electric lights, and hot and cold water.

Building railroads from ocean to ocean. The first railroad across the continent was the Union Pacific. It
was finished in 1869, four years after the war between
the North and South ended. Two companies started
building at the same time, one eastward from San Francisco, California, and the other westward from Omaha,
Nebraska. A road was being built from Chicago

to Omaha, and when these two new lines should meet, the railroad would stretch from ocean to ocean.

The government helps the railroad builders. In order to help the work, the government gave the railroad companies thirteen thousand acres of land along the right of way, for every mile of road that they built; and it lent them money besides. A race was started between the two companies. Each company wanted to build as many miles of railroad as possible in order to get more government land.

Difficulties of the railroad builders. But something more than land and money was needed to build a railroad. There must also be materials and men.

The difficulties at the western end were very great. Nearly all materials had to be shipped around Cape Horn, a distance of nineteen thousand miles. The engines were shipped in pieces and set up after they reached California. Sometimes they were six months on the way. Car wheels, rails, tools, and nearly everything made of iron had to come in the same way.

Troubles over labor caused the company to bring in Chinese workmen. They worked for a dollar a day and did much of the roughest and most dangerous part of the work. At one time the company had in its service eleven thousand Chinese laborers.

But the greatest difficulty of all was caused by the nature of the country. In some places the only way to go forward was to cut a shelf for the rails along the granite wall of a canyon. In other places tunnels must be blasted through the mountains. Snow storms blocked the valleys in winter and torrents destroyed the tracks in the spring. But in spite of everything the work pushed on.

Difficulties of another sort troubled the builders on the plains. They, too, had to bring their materials from far away. In the beginning the railroad to Omaha was not finished and they had to bring engines, rails, cars, and tools up the Missouri River on steamboats. Even ties and fuel had to be shipped from the east, for there was no timber on the plains.

The Indians try to stop the work. The builders had to be always on guard against the Indians, who attacked their camps and sometimes tore up the tracks. The Indians knew that white settlers would follow the railroads and take their hunting grounds, so they tried in every way to keep the railroads from being built.

The buffalo furnishes food. But how could the army of workmen get food? The buffalo answered that question. Thousands of these clumsy beasts roamed the plains from Montana to Texas, and the railroad companies hired hunters to kill them and keep the men supplied with fresh meat. One of the hunters, William F. Cody, killed more than four thousand buffalo in a year and a half. People called him "Buffalo Bill" all the rest of his life. In his book on the *Wild West* "Buffalo Bill" tells how the workmen were supplied with fresh meat and how he got his name. He says:*

"Twelve hundred men were employed in the work here, and as the Indians were very troublesome it became difficult to obtain enough fresh meat to feed such an army of workmen. To get over this difficulty

---

*Slightly adapted and abbreviated.

the contractors employed hunters to kill buffaloes. Buffalo meat is as good as the best beef.

"They made me a good offer to become their hunter, and I at once entered into a contract with them. They said that they would require about twelve buffaloes a day. As this was to be dangerous work, on account of the Indians, who were riding all over that section, I demanded a large salary. I would be obliged to go from five to ten miles from the road each day to hunt the buffaloes, accompanied by only one man with a light wagon for the transportation of the meat. They agreed to give me five hundred dollars a month.

"During my engagement as hunter for the company, a period of less than eighteen months, I killed four thousand two hundred and eighty buffaloes. It was at this time that the very appropriate name of 'Buffalo Bill' was given me by the road hands. It has stuck to me ever since. I had many exciting adventures with the Indians, as well as hairbreadth escapes.

"One day I suddenly saw a band of about thirty Indians nearly half a mile distant. I knew by the way they jumped on their horses that they had seen me.

"The only chance I had for my life was to make a run for it, and I immediately wheeled and started back toward the railroad. On reaching a ridge, I looked back and saw the Indians coming for me at full speed. They seemed to be gaining on me. When we had run about three miles further some eight or nine of the Indians were not over two hundred yards behind. One of their horses, a spotted animal, was gaining on me all the time.

"Buffalo Bill," the famous Indian fighter, hunter, and scout

"The Indian who was riding the spotted horse was armed with a rifle, and would occasionally send a bullet whistling along, sometimes striking the ground ahead of me. I saw that this fellow must be checked, or a stray bullet might hit me or my horse, so, suddenly stopping and quickly wheeling my horse around, I took deliberate aim at the Indian and his horse, hoping to hit one or the other, and fired. At the crack of my rifle, down went his horse. Not waiting to see if he recovered, I turned my horse and in a moment we were again fairly flying towards the railroad.

"The chase was kept up until we came within three miles of the railroad, where two companies of soldiers were stationed for the purpose of protecting the workmen from the Indians. One of the outposts saw the Indians chasing me across the prairie and gave the alarm. In a few minutes I saw, greatly to my delight, that the soldiers were galloping to my rescue as fast as they could mount their horses. When the Indians observed this, they turned and ran in the direction from which they had come. Before they had gone five miles we overtook and killed eight of their number."

The first railroad finished. The railroad building toward the east met the line building toward the west near Ogden, Utah, on May 10, 1869. There was great rejoicing, and the last rails were joined together with a golden spike.

The Union Pacific stretched across Nebraska, Wyoming, Utah, Nevada, and California and bound the new West to the old East with links of steel. In a few years branch lines ran north and south of the main line, and these branches brought other regions into connection with the Atlantic and the Pacific. In a few more years there were five railroads crossing the United States to the Pacific.

Changes made by the railroads. Villages sprang up along the railroads and grew into cities. Farms and ranches raised wheat and cattle, and the railroads carried the wheat and cattle to the eastern cities to feed the toiling thousands in machine shops and factories who could no longer raise their own food. At the same time the railroads carried to the West all the tools, machines, and store goods that the people on farms and ranches needed.

This exchange of the goods of one region for those of another shows us how all parts of the country depend upon one another. The people of the cities would starve without the meat and grain and vegetables and milk and butter and eggs that the farms and ranches raise. The farmers and ranchers would be very uncomfortable if they could not sell their things and get the goods of the cities. The railroads help all of us to get what we want when we want it.

But still the railroads do not haul all the freight nor carry all the passengers. The automobile truck has taken the place of the wagon, and the automobile and the airplane have taken the place of the horse and the stagecoach.

The Pony Express has gone the way of the ox-wagon. Fast trains run from St. Louis to San Francisco in three days. The airplane makes the flight in about eight hours. Telegraph and telephone messages cross the continent in the twinkling of an eye.

A SHORT STORY TO TELL

The early emigrants to the West passed over the plains and mountains beyond the Missouri River and settled on the Pacific coast in California, Oregon, and Washington.

In order that the people on the Pacific coast might get mail promptly from the East, the government started an overland mail service in 1857. The stage coaches which carried the mail also carried passengers.

The trip from St. Louis, Missouri, to San Francisco usually took twenty-four or twenty-five days.

In 1860, just before the beginning of the War between the North and the South, the Pony Express was established. The Pony Express riders carried mail from St. Louis to San Francisco in ten days. It cost five dollars to send a letter by the Pony Express. What does it cost now to send a letter from New York to California? The Pony Express came to an end when the telegraph lines were built across the continent at the end of 1861.

When miners and ranchmen began to settle in the mountains and plains the government built forts in many parts of the country and sent soldiers to the West to protect the people from the Indians. In order to carry supplies to the soldiers, the miners, the ranchmen, and the farmers, a great freighting business was built up. Most of the goods were carried in heavy wagons drawn by oxen.

The first railroad across the plains and mountains to California was largely built by the Union Pacific Company. This road was finished in 1869 and is called the Union Pacific.

WHAT THE MAP TELLS

1. Study the map on page 125 or the one on page 181. Look at a relief map in your geography. Tell why the first mail and passenger coaches were sent over the longest trail.

2. Point out the trail followed by the Pony Express. Why did it not follow the route of the Overland Mail?

3. Show which trail was closely followed by the first railroad. Why did it follow this trail?

4. Are there any western states that were not crossed by one of these western trails? If so name them.

ALONG THE WESTERN TRAILS

5. Make two lists: one of the things that helped the people to settle the West; one that tells the things that hindered them.

6. Do these names below make you think of stories? Choose one of the names and tell the story to the class.

"Jump-off"   Buffalo Bill
Societies of Vigilantes   Covered Wagon
Overland Mail   Union Pacific

7. Read one of the stories of the West in the books listed on page 180.

Chapter XV

THE SETTLEMENT OF MOUNTAINS AND PLAINS

THE RUSH TO THE MINES

The hunt for gold. The California miners found gold in the gravel and sand along the banks of mountain streams. The first discovery was made in 1848.

With his pick and shovel the miner dug up the earth and put it into the pan. He then poured water in the pan, and, with a whirling motion, washed the dirt loose from the fine grains of gold. The whirling motion splashed the water and dirt over the rim of the pan, but the gold, being heavier, sank to the bottom.

After about ten years it was no longer so easy to find rich deposits on the banks of the California streams. Then the miners began to say to themselves: "Well, there are other streams and other mountains in the West. They may be as rich as the California mines were in the beginning. Let's go and see." So "prospectors" hunting for gold began to explore regions that had never before felt the tread of a white man's foot.

The rush to Colorado. In 1858, just ten years after the first discovery in California, prospectors found rich mines on the mountain streams west of the present city of Denver. As soon as the news could get back to the settlements on the Missouri and Mississippi rivers a rush began.

Many thousands of gold seekers crossed the plains of western Kansas and eastern Colorado. Some of the travelers made a joke of the hard journey and painted on their wagon covers "Pike's Peak or Bust." The slogan meant that the emigrant had staked his last dollar on the chance of finding gold. If he failed, he would be penniless.

Denver, which is still the largest city on the plains, sprang up over night. Rich mining camps were formed at Central City, Georgetown, and Idaho Springs, near Denver.

Many of those who went to Colorado were disappointed. There was plenty of gold, but it was not so easy to get as it had been in California. Most of it was imbedded in the hard rocks of the mountains and could only be separated from the rock by the use of expensive machinery. The miners could not wash it out in pans.

So, many of the "Pike's Peak" miners lost hope of making their fortunes and recrossed the plains to the East. Some, however, continued to work the mines. Some wandered over the mountains hunting new mines. And still others settled down in the cool, fertile valleys and began to farm.

Thus we see how the mining rush led to the beginning of settlement in Colorado. The same thing happened in other western states.

The rush to Nevada. While the Pike's Peak rush was carrying its crowds of eager gold seekers to Colorado, a rich "strike" was made in the western part of the present state of Nevada. Here the mining towns of Carson City and Virginia City grew up. A few years later the Comstock mine was discovered in this region. It was one of the richest silver mines in the world.

The rush to Idaho, Montana, and Dakota. While the War between the North and the South was going on, gold was found in Idaho and Montana. Immediately there was a rush from the gold fields of California, Colorado, and Nevada. Thousands of "tenderfeet" flocked in also from the East. Almost in the twinkling of an eye camps grew into villages and villages into good sized towns. Lewiston and Pierce City were the largest settlements in Idaho; while Helena, Alder Gulch, and Bannock were the chief places in Montana. In 1876 gold was found in the Black Hills of Dakota, and here the famous mining city of Deadwood grew up.

Life in the gold diggings. Life at the mines was hard and dangerous. Men lived in the roughest of log cabins, in dug-outs, and in caves. They did their own cooking and washed their own clothes. They worked from daylight until dark. Then, to escape the loneliness of the night, many of them gathered in the saloons and gambling houses, drank strong whiskey, and lost the gold dust that they had gained by such painful labor during the day.

Desperadoes thronged the camps. Everybody carried a pistol and bowie knife for self-protection, but no man's life was safe. The criminals worked in gangs. Sometimes they were able to discover the hiding places in which prudent miners stored their dust. Sometimes they robbed the stage coaches by which the miners tried to ship their hard-earned gold to loved ones in the states.

Very often the officers were the leaders of the gangs and helped them to murder and steal. Usually, however, when honest men learned that they could not trust their officers they took the law into their own hands. They formed secret societies called Societies of Vigilantes. They hanged as many of the criminals as they could get their hands on and drove the rest away.

How the mining rushes led to settlement. Mining camps sprang up in many parts of the mountains. A promising strike brought miners flocking from all directions. Perhaps a few might "strike it rich" and settle down to work their claims, but the unsuccessful ones were ready to move on as soon as they heard of a new discovery somewhere else. In this way the mining rushes led to the opening up of the mountain country. They prepared the way for the ranchmen and the farmers.

A Texas cowboy. Cattle ranching started in Texas, and spread
over the western plains as far north as Canada.

THE COMING OF RANCHES AND FARMS

How the ranches came to the plains.   Most of the cattle
on the western ranches came originally from Texas.
During the War between the North and the South vast
herds ran wild on the Texas prairies.   At the end of
the war their owners began to drive them northward to
the railroad in Kansas and ship them to the packing
houses in Chicago.   Abilene, Wichita, and Dodge City
were called "cow towns" because it was at those places
that the trails from Texas struck the railroad.

Then men began to buy cattle and drive them to the

grassy plains of Colorado, Wyoming, and Montana. After they were fattened there they were shipped to market on the railroad or sold to the government to feed the Indians on the reservations. It was in this way that the great ranches began on the plains.

The long drive to the ranches. For the long drive to the ranches the cattle were divided into droves, or herds. The size of the herds differed. The smaller herds had about a thousand head of cattle in them. The larger ones contained as many as twenty-five hundred or three thousand head.

The herds took the trail in the spring, when the grass began to grow. They grazed along the way, and reached their northern homes in the early fall. In spite of their long journey, the cattle were sometimes fatter and heavier when they arrived than they were when they started. After grazing on the plains for a year or two they were shipped on the railroad to Chicago and sold for beef.

At the beginning of a drive the cowboys had a hard time keeping the cattle together. Some wanted to go too fast; some tried to lag behind; and others were always trying to stray away from the orderly herd. After a few days on the trail, however, they got into the habit of following the leaders and gave no trouble unless something unusual happened.

One thing that was always likely to cause trouble was the crossing of streams. There were no bridges and the cattle had to swim. Sometimes the cowboys could drive them into the water in small herds and get them across easily enough. But at other times the leaders would refuse to enter the water and then the whole herd would balk. In such cases there was nothing to be done except graze the cattle along the bank of the stream until they got over their fright.

The cowboy's greatest dread on the trail was a stampede. It usually came at night. Any sudden noise might rouse the cattle and make them nervous. A flash of lightning or a loud clap of thunder during a storm would almost surely start them to running.

When a storm threatened, the cowboys rode slowly around the herd and sang. They believed that singing helped to quiet the cattle. If a stampede started, they put spurs to their horses and dashed for the head of the herd. Once at the head, they shouted, waved their "slickers," fired their pistols, and did everything that they could to turn the leaders and get the herd to running in a circle. The cattle soon tired themselves out running in a circle and could then be bedded down again. If they got away, however, they scattered and often ran for many miles.

The life of the cowboy on the ranch. The first ranches on the plains had no fences. The cattle roamed wherever they pleased. But they had to have water and could usually be found near some creek or water hole. Perhaps the cattle of two or three, or even a half dozen, ranches might become mingled together on the unfenced plains.

It was the duty of the cowboys to round up the cattle twice a year, in the spring and in the fall. At the round-ups they separated the cattle of each ranch from those of the others and drove them to their home ranges.

Twice a year the cowboys rounded up the cattle on the open ranges so that owners might take out those they wanted put on the home ranges.

They branded the young calves with the owner's brand. This branding was necessary to enable them to know who owned the calves when they grew up. It was easy to tell who owned a calf because it always followed its mother and the mother was branded.

While some of the cowboys were branding the calves, others separated the beeves from the herd and drove them to the railroad, to be shipped to market and sold.

When the cowboys were not working at the round-ups they had many other things to do. They rode from place to place looking after the grazing cattle and try-ing to keep them out of trouble. There was always danger from cattle thieves, called "rustlers." Some-times an animal bogged in the mud or quicksand at the watering places and had to be dragged out by the horses. After the ranchmen began to fence their ranches with barbed wire some of the cowboys had to spend part of their time riding along the fences and repairing breaks and cuts.

The hardest work came in the winter. When the water froze over, the cowboys had to break holes in the ice so the cattle could drink. They had to look after the weaker animals and keep them from straying away from the shelter of the gulches and canyons. The worse the weather became, the more the cowboys had to ride.

But there was one winter job that the cowboys always enjoyed. That was hunting wolves. The big prairie wolves were called lobos. They were as large as a big dog and two or three of them could kill a beef. They liked only fresh meat, and could not often be deceived by poisoned meat. The cowboys had to hunt them down and kill them.

The wolf hunt usually began just about daybreak. The wolves would be returning then to their dens. The cowboys would try to head them off and keep them in the open prairies. There they could run them down and either shoot them or rope them. But sometimes they used dogs to chase the wolves to their dens. Then one of the men would crawl into the hole with a lighted candle and shoot at the shining eyes.

There is an amusing story about two cowboys named Charley and Frank. They found a den with a very small entrance and neither of them wanted to go into it. They drew straws to decide the question and Charley lost, so he had to go in. "With sixshooter in hand he crawled in until he could see the eyes of the wolf gleaming at him. Up came the sixshooter and the roar of the shot shook dust and loose dirt from the walls and dinned in the cowboy's ears.

"The shot missed, and the lobo, seeing a gleam of light over Charley's back, made a break for the outside. The space was too small for her to pass through, and she became wedged between Charley's back and the roof of the cave. Frantic with fear, she began scratching away in an attempt to dig out, and every scratch carried away some of the cowboy's clothes. Finally she dug through and Frank shot her as she came out. Nine pups were found in the den."*

The coming of the farmers.   First came the miners, then the ranchmen, and finally the farmers. Congress passed a law giving anybody who wished it a hundred and sixty acres of land for a homestead. All that was necessary to get the land was to build a cabin and live on the land five years.

The ranchmen did not want the farmers to settle near them. They called them "nesters" and tried to drive them away. But the "nesters" kept coming. They built fences to keep the ranch cattle from eating their crops. Wherever they could do so they selected land in the fertile mountain valleys, where they had plenty of water. Then they began to push out on the plains, away from the mountains but close enough to the streams to bring water to their farms in irrigation ditches.

Even where there were no streams they learned a sort of dry-land farming. They drilled wells and put

*Slightly adapted from J. Evetts Haley, *The XIT Ranch of Texas.*

up windmills to pump water for the family and for the horses and cows, but they raised their crops by carefully cultivating the land and taking the utmost advantage of the scattering showers that fell during the spring and summer.

In this way people spread slowly over the mountains and plains. Cities and towns grew up. Schools were built. And before many years had passed half a dozen western states were asking for admission to the Union.

The settlement of Utah. The first of the states to be settled on the far western plains was Utah. It was one of the last, however, to be admitted to the Union.

Utah was settled by the members of the Mormon Church under their leader, Brigham Young. In the summer of 1847 they started a settlement on the shore of the Great Salt Lake. Three years later there were eleven thousand people in the valley. They were farmers and cattle raisers. Brigham Young would not let them go to the mines, but they made money by staying at home and trading with the people who crossed the plains to California, Nevada, and Idaho. Utah quickly became one of the most prosperous of all the western settlements.

The rush to Oklahoma. The state that we now call Oklahoma was set aside by Congress as a home for the civilized Indians. But all the land was not needed by the Indians, so Congress bought some of it back and opened it to white settlers.

President Harrison gave out a message saying that the selection of the land for homesteads should begin at twelve o'clock on April 22, 1889. The land was

A vast open prairie was changed almost in a twinkling to a land of thriving farms and towns, when Oklahoma was opened for settlement.

divided into tracts of a hundred and sixty acres each. Any man or woman who first selected a tract and applied at the government land office could get the tract free for a homestead.

In order that all might have a fair chance, guards were placed around the land and the people were warned not to go in and pick out their land before the signal was given. If anybody broke the rules and the officers found it out, he was not allowed to have any land.

The news that the government was giving away land was printed in the newspapers, and thousands of people

Guthrie, Oklahoma, four years after the country was opened. Settlers raced for the free land, and towns of tents became towns of wood and brick in a few weeks or at most in a very few months.

began to move toward Oklahoma. Some of them already owned land, but thought they might get better land in Oklahoma. Some had no land and looked upon this opportunity to get a free homestead as the chance of a lifetime.

On the twenty-second of April there were about fifty thousand people waiting for the signal to begin the run. It was before the time of automobiles and airplanes. Some were in wagons and carriages, some were on horseback, and some were on foot. Many who had come in carriages unhitched their fleetest horses and mounted them for the race.

As the hour of twelve approached the signal officer got ready. He rode to a high point of ground from which he could be seen a long way. "At precisely twelve o'clock he raised the bugle to his lips and gave the signal blast, long and loud, waving and dropping the flag at the same moment. Then began the race for homes."

When the government counted the people about a year after the run began Oklahoma had more than two hundred and fifty thousand inhabitants. You can see from these figures how rapidly people moved into the country that seemed so full of promise.

THE LAST STAND OF THE INDIANS

The Plains Indians. Five important groups, or nations, of Indians made their homes on the plains. The Sioux Nation lived in the northern part of the plains, in Minnesota, North and South Dakota, and Montana. Sometimes they wandered into other regions. The Cheyennes and Arapahos lived mostly in Colorado, Wyoming, and Utah. The Comanches and Apaches were at home on the plains of Texas, New Mexico, and Arizona. Besides these five nations there were many smaller tribes.

All the plains Indians were good horsemen and are sometimes called horse Indians. They moved their camps from time to time. They rarely planted any crops, and lived chiefly on buffalo meat. They ate fresh meat in the summer, when the herds were grazing on the grass, and dried meat in winter, when the buffaloes moved south.

Why the Indians opposed the white settlers. It is easy to understand why the plains Indians opposed the settlement of the whites. The whites ruined the hunting grounds. They killed or drove off the buffaloes and other game.

The Indians hunted to get food and killed no more of the wild animals than they needed. But the white men hunted for fun. They shot the buffaloes by the hundreds just to see them tumble. Occasionally two hunters would make a bet and dash into a herd to see how many each of them could kill in a day. The one who killed the most won the bet.

What really put an end to the buffaloes, however, was hunting them for their skins. Bands of hunters went out with wagons and skinners. They shot the buffaloes day after day, while the skinners removed the pelts and loaded them on wagons to be sold to the tanneries in the east. After a few years of such hunting the buffaloes disappeared.

The Indians knew very well what would happen to them when the buffaloes were all gone. They would either have to change their ways of living or starve. So they tried to drive the white settlers away before the buffaloes were killed off.

Indian raids. These Indians of the plains were cruel and merciless. They could fight desperately when they wanted to, but they preferred to pounce upon scattered settlements and lonely ranch houses when the men were away and only the women and children at home. Then they would torture the women to death, kill the children, burn the houses, and steal the horses and cattle.

Such attacks as these caused the white people to hate and fear the Indians, and led them to treat the Indians almost as cruelly as the Indians treated the whites.

The government tries to keep the Indians on reservations.
The government tried to protect both the settlers and
the Indians by putting the Indians on reservations.
Congress set aside land in a great number of places for
the different tribes, and appointed agents to live among
the Indians and give them food and clothing and blankets, and also rifles and ammunition for hunting.

These parts of the country that were set aside, or re-
served, for the Indians were called reservations. The
government agents tried to teach the Indians to do a little farming. But the plains Indians did not want to
farm. They wanted to roam freely over the plains and
take their food where they found it. So, even after
they agreed to live on the reservations, they kept breaking away. The government would send soldiers to
drive them back and when the soldiers and the Indians
met there would nearly always be war.

Indian wars. We cannot study here about all the battles between the Indians and the soldiers. It is necessary, however, to learn the story of two or three of
them in order to understand how the plains were made
safe for white settlers. Both the Indians and the soldiers endured terrible suffering. Sometimes it seemed
that the soldiers were as cruel as the Indians. They
said that the Indians felt no gratitude for kind treatment and that the only way to make them behave was
to punish them severely and "give them a taste of their
own medicine."

The fight on the Republican River. Colonel George
A. Forsyth, with a little company of fifty men, had one
of the most thrilling battles ever fought on the plains.

The scene of the battle was a small island in the Republican River, in northern Kansas, and the time was September, 1868. Colonel Forsyth wrote a report of the battle to General Sheridan, and we can read the story almost in his own words.

"Our equipment," he wrote, "was simple. We had a blanket apiece, saddle and bridle, lariat and picket pin to tie the horses at night, a canteen, a haversack, butcher knife, tin plate, tin cup, a repeating rifle, and a Colt's revolver. Each man had a hundred and forty rounds of rifle ammunition and thirty rounds of revolver ammunition. In addition we had a pack train of four mules carrying camp kettles, picks and shovels. We should need them in case it became necessary to dig for water. We had also four thousand extra rounds of ammunition.

"Just at the first flash of dawn we heard the thud of unshod horses' feet, and a few seconds later we caught sight of the waving feathers in the war bonnet of a mounted warrior.

"I saw at once that their intention was to stampede our horses, for they dashed forward on their ponies, rattling dried hides, beating Indian drums, and yelling at the top of their lungs. It was too late for that, however, as nearly every soldier already had his horse's lariat wrapped around his left arm and his rifle grasped in both hands.

"By this time it was light enough to see dimly. We were surrounded by a thousand Indians. I ordered my men to lead their horses to the little island out in the river and tie them in a circle to the bushes.

"Placing our extra boxes of ammunition on four of the saddles, we waded out to the island. Then the men dropped to the ground and began digging pits with their butcher knives and tin plates.

"Our movement to the island was unexpected, and for a few moments seemed to puzzle the Indians. As soon as they began to understand what it meant, they were wild with rage. They poured in a heavy fire upon us, killing and wounding several of the men.

"The warriors were commanded by a gigantic chief. I recognized him as Roman Nose, of the Northern Cheyennes. They swept toward us in a furious charge. The warriors were entirely naked and hideously painted. Their hair was braided and their scalp locks were ornamented with feathers. They rode bare-backed, with only a horsehair lariat wrapped twice around their horses and passing lightly over each knee.

"We met the charging warriors with volley after volley. At the sixth volley Roman Nose and his horse went down together. A few of the Indians reached the foot of our little island, but there we met them with our rapid revolver fire and they gave it up."

Colonel Forsyth then tells how the fight went on for more than a week. His own leg was broken and he had a bullet wound in his head. Nearly half of his men were either killed or wounded. They had nothing to eat but the flesh of their dead horses. But at last they were rescued.

"On the morning of the ninth day one of the men lying near me suddenly sprang up, and, shading his eyes with his hand, shouted that he saw soldiers and an ambulance approaching. The strain was over. It was Colonel Carpenter with a troop of the Tenth Cavalry."

General Custer's last battle.   After twenty years of warfare and more than a hundred battles, most of the Indians agreed to live on the government reservations. But two of the fiercest Sioux chiefs refused to make peace. These two, Crazy Horse and Sitting Bull, preferred to keep up their wild life on the Montana plains.

In the summer of 1876 the government sent three armies to hunt down Crazy Horse and Sitting Bull and force them to go to the reservations. One force of about seven hundred men was led by General George A. Custer, the most dashing Indian fighter in the United States Army.

Custer discovered the Indians on the Little Big Horn River in southern Montana. Their village extended for several miles along the west side of the river. He divided his force to attack it. He himself with two hundred and twenty-five men rode down the river to strike the Indians at the lower end of the village. The remainder of his force, more than four hundred men, was to attack the village at its upper end.

The larger force, under Major Reno, was driven back by the Indians. The Indians then turned on Custer and crossed the river to meet him. He was several miles down the river and out of sight of the troops that Major Reno commanded. Though Custer did not know it, Crazy Horse and Sitting Bull had united their warriors and the Indians had ten times as many men as there were in Custer's little command.

General Custer's last stand

The Indians were as well armed as the soldiers. They were wild with rage and excitement and the battle could end in but one way. Not a single white man escaped with his life. It was the greatest victory that the Indians ever won over the soldiers.

Two days later reinforcements came up. They were too late to save Custer and his brave men, but they could carry on the war against the Indians. A few months later Crazy Horse surrendered and led his warriors to the reservation. Sitting Bull escaped to Canada, where the soldiers could not follow him. Five years after the death of Custer he, too, surrendered.

The end of the Indian wars. The great Indian wars were over in the north by 1877, but in the south the Indians continued to give trouble. The Apaches repeatedly slipped away from their reservation in Arizona and took the warpath under the famous chief Geronimo. Geronimo's last battle was fought in 1886. The soldiers followed him into Mexico and compelled him to surrender. The government then imprisoned him in Fort Pickens at Pensacola, Florida. Later he was removed to Oklahoma, where he was finally released. His fighting days were over.

The history of the Indians makes a sad and tragic story. They loved their wild homes and fought to preserve them. They did not want to adopt the ways of the white men. They did not want to dig gold out of the earth. They did not want to farm. They did not want to raise cattle. They wanted to rove freely over the mountains and plains and take their food from the swarming wild herds. The white men wanted to build homes, establish ranches, and cultivate farms. The two ways of living could not go on together. Either the Indians must change their ways or the white people must stay out of the country.

The government tried to treat the Indians fairly and kindly by putting them on the reservations. When they broke away and went on the warpath, killing the white settlers and destroying the settlements, there was nothing to do but send the soldiers after them and force them back to the reservations. The management of the Indians was a difficult problem. No doubt the government made some mistakes, but it is hard to see how it could have settled the problem except in the way that it did.

A SHORT STORY TO TELL

West of the Mississippi River lie the high plains and the Rocky Mountains. White people were just beginning to settle in this region in 1861 when the War between the North and the South began.

The miners led the way into the mountain regions. Their experience in California caused them to think that they might find gold on the banks of the rushing streams. Prospectors swarmed into Colorado, Nevada, Idaho, Montana, Wyoming, and South Dakota. Many mines were discovered and much gold and silver was taken out. But the most important thing that these miners did was to begin the settlement of these states.

On the heels of the miners came the ranchmen and farmers. Large cattle ranches were established on the plains, where cattle were raised for the growing cities in the East, and even in Europe; for the packing houses shipped a great deal of beef across the ocean.

The farmers who were fortunate enough to get land near the streams watered their crops by irrigation. Those who were unable to get land on a stream learned a way of dry-land farming. By cultivating the land carefully and selecting the seeds for the crop that they wanted to plant they could get along with very little water. They fenced their land with barbed wire and drilled wells for water. They raised the water from the deep wells with pumps run by windmills.

The Indians saw with dread and horror the growth of the white settlements. They knew that the whites would soon destroy the game animals and force the Indians to live on the government reservations or starve. They made raids on the settlements, robbing the ranches and farms, burning the houses, and torturing and killing the whites wherever they found them. The government sent soldiers to protect the settlers and there was war with the Indians for nearly twenty years.

WORD PICTURES

1. Choose one of the suggestions below and prepare to give a good description before the class.

Describe the way in which cattle were taken from the plains to market.

Describe the race for land in Oklahoma.

Describe the struggle between the white man and the Indian for control of the plains.

FAMOUS SPEECHES

2. Make a speech that an Indian chief might have made to the President of the United States in which he tells the President how the Indians feel about the white men.

3. Make a speech that the President might have made in answer. He would explain why the white men were there, and what the government was doing for the Indians.

HOW DO YOU FEEL ABOUT IT?

4. Write a paragraph or two in which you tell how you feel about the way the Indians were treated by the white man. Give reasons for your feelings.

NEW WORDS TO CONQUER

5. See if you can give the correct meaning for each of these words. If you miss a word write it on the blackboard and the next pupil will continue. When everyone has had a turn look up the words that are on the board and write each in a sentence.

rustler	heeves
lobo	"nester"
round-up	branding
stampede	prospector
tannery	pelt
reservation	lariat

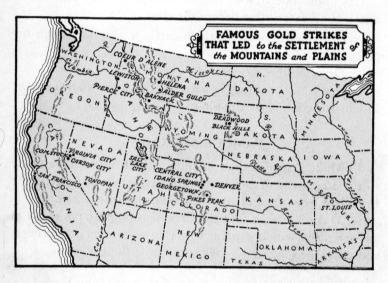

FAMOUS GOLD STRIKES THAT LED *to the* SETTLEMENT *of the* MOUNTAINS *and* PLAINS

UNIT SIX

SOME MAKERS OF MODERN AMERICA

We shall read in the following chapters about some of the men and women who have helped to make our country what it is.

We cannot study in one book the lives of all the men and women who have been leaders in the making of our nation. There are so many of them that the book would be too big. So we shall have to choose only a few of those who have taken the lead in different kinds of work.

We shall let four men represent the leaders in government, two Republicans and two Democrats. The Democrats are Grover Cleveland and Woodrow Wilson; the Republicans, Theodore Roosevelt and Herbert Hoover.

Three other leaders of whom we shall read are Mark Twain, Samuel Gompers, and Luther Burbank.

Mark Twain worked his way up from a job as press boy in his brother's printing shop to be the most popular and best-loved writer of American literature. His brother writers called him the "king."

Samuel Gompers came from London to the United States as an immigrant boy. He devoted his life to the improvement of the condition of the laboring people. He started a great union of working people called the American Federation of Labor, and was its president for thirty-five years. The poor immigrant boy became the adviser of the President of the United States, and many thousands of people are happier today because of his work.

Luther Burbank was the "wizard of plants." He began his life work as a market gardener in Massachusetts. He grew better vegetables than the other gardeners, and became known especially for his fine Burbank potatoes. He moved to California and started his gardening on a great scale. By careful study he developed plums and berries more delicious than had ever been grown before, and his daisies and lilies seemed to be the work of a magician. Perhaps you would like to know how he brought about some of his magical effects.

In Chapter XX you may read about some of the things that women have done to make our nation what it is. Not so very long ago it was thought that the proper work of women was to keep the house, darn the stockings, and nurse the children. When we look around us today we see women doing nearly all the things that men can do. How did this change come about?

BOOKS THAT TELL YOU MORE ABOUT THE PEOPLE IN
UNIT SIX

Slusser, E. Y., and Others, *Stories of Luther Burbank* (Charles Scribner's Sons).

Roosevelt, Theodore, *Theodore Roosevelt's Letters to His Children* (Charles Scribner's Sons).

Baldwin, James, *American Book of Golden Deeds* (American Book Company).

Parkman, M. R., *Heroines of Service* (D. Appleton-Century Company).

Chapter XVI

FOUR LEADERS IN GOVERNMENT

Grover Cleveland

THE RIVALRY OF THE PARTIES

The Republicans and the Democrats. In Chapter II we learned how our government was made. The government is formed of the President, the Congress, the courts, and many thousands of less important officers.

All of the people cannot take part in the work of the government, because they have other work to do, so they elect officers to run the government for them.

The men and women who vote and elect the officers are divided into parties. Those political parties are somewhat like clubs. Each party tries to elect some of its own members to run the government. The two strongest parties in the United States are the Republicans and the Democrats.

The success of the Republicans. The Republicans have been most successful in electing officers. Since the death of President Lincoln in 1865 until 1936, there have been sixteen Presidents. Three of these were Democrats and all the others were Republicans.

The list given here tells the names of the Presidents, the dates of their service and the state from which each was elected.

Name	In Office	Elected from
Andrew Johnson	April, 1865–1869	Tennessee
Ulysses S. Grant	1869–1877	Illinois
Rutherford B. Hayes	1877–1881	Ohio
James A. Garfield	March–September, 1881	Ohio
Chester A. Arthur	September, 1881–1885	New York
Grover Cleveland	1885–1889	New York
Benjamin Harrison	1889–1893	Indiana
Grover Cleveland	1893–1897	New York
William McKinley	1897–September, 1901	Ohio
Theodore Roosevelt	September, 1901–1909	New York
William H. Taft	1909–1913	Ohio
Woodrow Wilson	1913–1921	New Jersey
Warren G. Harding	1921–August, 1923	Ohio
Calvin A. Coolidge	August, 1923–1929	Massachusetts
Herbert Hoover	1929–1933	California
Franklin D. Roosevelt	1933–	New York

We cannot study here the work of each of these men, so we shall learn something about two of the Democrats who have been President and about two of the Republicans. The Democratic Presidents whom we shall read about were Grover Cleveland and Woodrow Wilson. The Republicans were Theodore Roosevelt and Herbert Hoover.

GROVER CLEVELAND

Boyhood. Grover Cleveland was born in a village in New Jersey, on March 18, 1837. His father was a Presbyterian minister with a large family and a small salary, so that Grover had to go to work and earn his own living at an age when most boys are in school. But he liked to work, and he liked to study, so that his having to work did not keep him from getting a very good education.

First he worked in a grocery store, running errands, sweeping the floor, and, as he grew older, waiting on people. When he was seventeen he got a place in a law office. Here he swept the floor, copied letters, took care of important papers, and did whatever odd jobs there were to do. Between times he studied law, and when he was twenty-two he became a lawyer in the city of Buffalo, New York.

Early manhood. Cleveland's mind was slow and plodding. He feared nobody, and nobody could tell him what he ought to do. He thought things out for himself. When he had once made up his mind in an important matter he hardly ever changed it. Almost the last words that he spoke before he died were: "I have tried so hard to do right."

People like such a man, and they liked Cleveland. They took their law business to him, and he served them faithfully and honestly. But he was a quiet, modest man, not a "mixer," and for a long time very few people knew him. Apparently he did not seek office or public life.

When Cleveland was thirty-three years old, he was elected sheriff of his county. This election brought him into politics, but he carried on the duties of this office as he had carried on his law business. He was still quiet and plodding and faithful. People trusted him, but they still thought very little about him. Eleven years later they elected him mayor of the city of Buffalo. Then people began to learn about him.

Rapid rise to the presidency. When he was elected mayor of Buffalo (1881) Cleveland was forty-four years old, and the world was soon to hear of him. He managed the business of the city as he did the business of his law office, faithfully, and honestly. He worked hard. He acted as if all the people of the city were his friends, coming to his office for help; and he worked to help them.

The next year the Democrats needed a man to run for governor of New York. They chose the mayor of Buffalo, and elected him. The day he was elected Cleveland wrote his brother, "I want to do well, but I do not know whether I can do what I wish. If mother were alive, I should feel much safer. I have always thought that her prayers had much to do with my success."

As governor, he carried on the duties of the office as he had done his law business. He tried to do right by all the people of the state, and he did his work so well that the Democrats decided to try to make him President. He was working in the governor's office when some of his friends outside fired a cannon to celebrate his nomination. One of his assistants called his attention to it. "Well, anyhow," Cleveland answered, "we'll finish up this work." That was the sort of man he was; always trying to "finish up this work," and always doing it himself, trying to do it right.

He was elected President of the United States, and took office on March 4, 1885. Four years later he was defeated by Harrison, the Republican candidate. But in 1892 he was elected a second time, and took up the duties of the presidency for another four years, in March, 1893.

In the presidency Cleveland did as he had done in all his other offices. His motto was: "Public office is a public trust." He meant by this motto that it was his duty as President to serve all the people of the United States as faithfully and honestly as he would serve a friend who brought a case to his law office. He tried to run the government cheaply so that the people would not have to pay high taxes, and he vetoed, without fear or favor, several hundred bills passed by Congress during his term of office intended to give pensions to persons he thought had not earned them.

Two acts of President Cleveland during his second term show his courage and independence.

First, he used soldiers of the regular United States Army to stop rioting by railroad men who had gone on a strike. The men not only refused to run the trains but tried to prevent other workmen from running them. The President said, "The United States mail must go through," and he ordered the Army to clear the way. The riots were over and the country at peace within twenty-four hours.

Second, he warned England that it must not take by force a piece of territory in South America that was claimed by Venezuela. In a special message to Congress, he gave England to understand that the United States would assist Venezuela if the English government continued its plans to take the territory. England did not want to go to war, but the British honestly believed that the territory belonged to them. Finally it agreed to submit the question to a court. In this way the dispute was settled without war.

When President Cleveland went out of office in 1897, he went to live at Princeton, New Jersey, near his boyhood home. There he became a teacher in Princeton University.

President Cleveland was a great hunter and fisherman. One of his most delightful books is named *Fishing and Hunting Sketches.*

THEODORE ROOSEVELT

Boyhood. Theodore Roosevelt was born in New York City, October 27, 1858. Unlike Grover Cleveland, he was born into a rich and well known family. His uncles and grandfathers had been in the politics, business, and social life of New York for more than a hundred years before his birth. His mother's family was as well known in Georgia as his father's family was in New York.

Young Roosevelt had all but one thing to make him a happy boy. The one thing that he lacked was health. His eyes were weak, his body was puny, and sometimes he could hardly get his breath on account of asthma.

Because of his poor health and weak eyes, he did not go to school with other children, but was taught at home.

The boy wished to grow strong. He rowed and swam in Long Island Sound. He tramped and lived most of the time out of doors. He learned to box and wrestle. By the time he was ready to go to Harvard University he was as strong as any of his classmates, and was the best boxer in his class. But he did not stop his outdoor exercises. He continued to walk and ride horseback, he boxed and wrestled and played tennis, and as he grew older he became a great hunter.

Student, cowboy, and writer of books. Roosevelt always studied hard. He not only studied books, he wrote them. A few years after he graduated from Harvard he published a history of the War of 1812. He loved the West with its history of pioneers, scouts, Indians and frontier life, and he wrote a history of the West in four volumes. He bought a ranch in North Dakota, and lived for several years the life of a cowboy. He wrote a book on ranch life.

Theodore Roosevelt

Altogether, he wrote more than twenty volumes, besides a great number of magazine articles.

Soldier. When Roosevelt was forty years old something happened which made him famous and started him on the road to the presidency. The United

States went to war with Spain to help the people of
Cuba, whom Spain had governed badly. Roosevelt
made up a cavalry regiment of Rough Riders at San
Antonio, Texas, and joined the army.

The Rough Riders were cowboys, ranchmen, big
game hunters, rangers, engineers, and business men
who wanted to fight for their country. They were
all fine horsemen. That is why they were called
Rough Riders. In Cuba the Rough Riders, led by
Colonel Roosevelt, took part in some of the most
dangerous fighting. Their charge up San Juan Hill
was the most thrilling event of the fighting on land.

This war between Spain and the United States is
called the Spanish-American War.

Rise to the presidency. The war was soon over,
and Roosevelt returned to New York one of the most
famous men in the United States. All the newspapers were talking about him. He was first elected
governor of New York, and served two years. Then
he was elected Vice-President. When President
McKinley was killed by a half-insane man in 1901,
Roosevelt became President. He was again elected
in 1904. He served altogether seven and a half
years—from September, 1901, until March, 1909.

Saving the forests and streams. President Roosevelt
had a great love for the mountains and plains, the
forests and streams, and the wild game of the woods.
He believed that the forests should be saved. Saw-
mills should not be allowed to cut down trees and
leave nothing but dead stumps and rotting brush
piles. Forest fires started by careless campers should

be prevented. He believed that streams should be dammed and the waters used to irrigate dry land and make it into useful farms.

By the advice of the President, Congress passed laws turning the forests on the government lands into national parks. People cannot cut down trees in these parks without permission of a forest officer. Forest guards put out fires and keep people from hunting game in the government forests. At the same time Congress took steps to build dams and save the water in the western streams for use in irrigating the land. It also passed laws limiting the mining of coal and the taking of oil from government lands.

The object of all such laws is to save the natural beauties and riches of the country and turn them to the enjoyment of all the people. We owe President Roosevelt a great debt of thanks for saving so many forests and streams.

Building the Panama Canal. It was due to President Roosevelt that the Panama Canal was built. The canal connects the Atlantic and the Pacific Oceans. Ships can now sail from the Atlantic to the Pacific or from the Pacific to the Atlantic coast without making the long and expensive voyage around South America. As a result, freight rates are cheaper and prices are lower on many goods than they would be if these goods could not be shipped through the canal. The canal is a great benefit to the rest of the world as well as to the United States. (See picture and map on following pages).

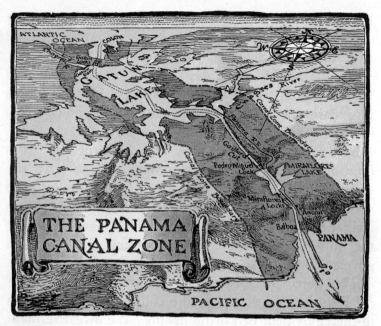

THE PANAMA CANAL ZONE

Hunter and explorer. When his second term as President was over, Roosevelt sailed for a hunting trip to Africa. When he was a boy he had traveled with his father in Egypt and had made a collection of Egyptian birds. He was now going to collect skins of African beasts for the National Museum at Washington. He wrote a book called *African Game Trails* which tells about his adventures in Africa. Later he went on a hunting and exploring trip to South America, and wrote a book about that.

His character. There have been but few Presidents so well known and so well liked as Theodore Roosevelt. While he was President he visited every state in the Union. He mixed with all sorts of people

The Panama Canal shows how man is changing the face of the earth for his convenience.

and wrote letters by the thousands. Millions of people who never saw him read his books and his magazine articles, and affectionately called him "Teddy." It has been said: "He was an easterner in the East, a westerner in the West, and he was, in fact, half southerner."

His family life. But we cannot fully know the charm of President Roosevelt's character without following him into his home and seeing him there with his wife and children. We can get the best picture of his home life by reading the letters that he wrote to his children. He had six children, two daughters and four sons, and he wrote regularly to all of them when he was away from them. These letters have been printed in a book.

To the youngest boy, only six, he would write about the birds and the animals that he saw in the woods. He would draw pictures in the letters showing Br'er Terrapin and Br'er Rabbit, and funny pictures of himself playing tennis and boxing.

To the older children he would write about his trips. Once he made a long trip from Washington to San Antonio, Texas, where there was to be a meeting of his old rough riders. He wrote that he was delighted with the warm, friendly way the people of Texas treated him.

From San Antonio he went to Oklahoma. There his friends had arranged for him to go on a wolf hunt. One of his letters told about the hunt. They killed seventeen wolves, three coons, and a number of rattlesnakes. One wolf led the dogs a chase of nine miles and President Roosevelt and the leader of the hunt were the only members of the party who were with the dogs when the wolf was caught.

The President thought the professional hunter, the leader, "a really wonderful fellow." He had a way of catching the wolves alive. When the dogs had a wolf rounded up, he would jump off his horse and thrust his gloved hand between the wolf's jaws in such a way as to keep it from biting him. The President wrote: "He caught one wolf alive, tied it up and holding it on the saddle, followed his dogs in a seven-mile run and helped kill another wolf."

From the wolf hunt President Roosevelt went on to Colorado to hunt bear. In a letter to his daughter Ethel he told how the people from the ranches came out to his camp with milk and eggs or a cake "for the President." A dozen or so of the men insisted on going along to see him shoot a bear, and he was very proud to write that he did kill one after an all-day ride.

He wrote about the pets that people sent to the White House, about his horseback rides with Mrs. Roosevelt in the parks, about his wrestling lessons with a Japanese wrestler, about the stories that he read to the children at night.

Roosevelt died in 1919. He was a great man and a great President.

WOODROW WILSON

Boyhood. Woodrow Wilson was born at Staunton, Virginia, in 1856. His father, like Cleveland's father, was a Presbyterian preacher. All his early life was passed in the South.

Teacher and university president. Like Cleveland, he became a lawyer, but he preferred to be a teacher, and, again like Cleveland, he taught in Princeton University. Finally he became president of the University.

All his life Wilson was a student and a writer. He wrote books on history and biography and on government. Next to Roosevelt, Wilson wrote more books than any other President.

His rise to the presidency. In 1910 the Democrats elected Wilson governor of New Jersey. Under his

direction, the legislature passed many laws for the
good of the people. He thought he knew what the
people wanted. He tried to give them what they wanted
and they liked him for it.

Wilson made such a fine record as governor of New
Jersey that the Democrats elected him President. He
took office in March, 1913, and served eight years,
until March, 1921.

As President, Wilson tried to carry on the government for the good of all the people, as he had done

while governor of New
Jersey. As a result of the
laws that he got Congress to
pass, the "common people"
of the United States were
helped by the government
as they had never been
helped before.

Wilson and the World War.
In August, 1914, a little more
than a year after President
Wilson took office, the whole

Woodrow Wilson

world was shocked by the beginning of a war in Europe.
The war spread quickly and soon nearly every important nation in the world was fighting.

On one side were Germany, Austria, Turkey, and
some smaller countries. On the other side were France,
Belgium, Russia, Italy, and England, with many
smaller nations. All the warring countries were our
friends, and President Wilson tried to get them to
make peace. But they would not make peace.

American and French soldiers were greeted with joy by the people of St. Mihiel when the town was regained for France.

Then President Wilson said that the United States would take no part in the war; that it would not take sides. But as the war went on, it became harder and harder for the United States to stay out. Both England and Germany did things that injured the United States, but, of the two, Germany's acts were the worse. Germany allowed its submarines to sink American ships and caused in that way the death of many American citizens.

An American dispatch bearer carrying a message through enemy territory, on the battle front in northern France.

Finally, on April 6, 1917, the United States joined in the war against Germany and the countries that were fighting on its side. The United States fought on the side of England and France.

The United States at war with Germany. At once the whole United States became a training camp to train officers, to drill soldiers, to teach flying and to make an immense army of fighting men. Soon our ships were carrying thousands of men to France. By the summer of 1918 the United States had more than a million men in France and four million more were getting ready to go there.

The warships of the United States steamed back and forth across the ocean, guarding the vessels that carried soldiers and supplies. The navy worked hand in hand with the army.

In the summer of 1918 the Americans did their first important fighting. During June and July they took part in the second Battle of the Marne. This battle stopped the last German drive on Paris. At the beginning of this battle, which lasted more than two months, the American marines did such wonderful fighting at Belleau Wood that the French government changed the name of the little forest to the "Wood of the Marine Brigade."

American soldiers also captured St. Mihiel (San Meyel) in September, 1918. And they fought in the long, desperate Battle of the Argonne Forest in October and November of 1918. Slowly the German army was pushed back.

Marshal Ferdinand Foch

The entire army of the United States was under the command of General John J. Pershing. It was the largest army that the United States ever had in the field. General Pershing worked with the French and English commanders. In fact, at the close of the war all of the armies that were fighting Germany were under the French commander, General Ferdinand Foch (Fosh).

The entrance of the United States into the war, with all its strength and its fresh, powerful army and navy, brought Germany to peace. The fighting stopped at eleven o'clock on November 11, 1918, since known as Armistice Day. Eight months later, on June 28, 1919, the treaty of peace was signed.

President Wilson tries to make a lasting peace. President Wilson wanted to make a peace treaty that would never be broken. He wanted to end war forever. For that reason he went to Paris and took part in the talks

General John J. Pershing

that led to the treaty. He tried to arrange a fair treaty but, in spite of all that he could do, the treaty was too hard on Germany and later it had to be changed.

President Wilson got all the countries that had been fighting to agree that in future they would try to settle their quarrels without war. They formed what is called the League of Nations and signed a pledge to try to stop war forever. Our government was willing to sign the pledge against war, but it did not want to join the League of Nations. President Wilson was greatly disappointed, because he believed that the only way to make the world safe was for our country to join the League of Nations. He wore himself out traveling and making speeches, trying to persuade the people of the United States to join the League. He was stricken with paralysis, and remained a broken and feeble invalid until he died on February 3, 1924.

Herbert Hoover as a boy, and the house at West Branch, Iowa, where he was born.

HERBERT HOOVER

Boyhood and education. Herbert Hoover was born on a farm in Iowa, August 10, 1874. He was only four years old when his father died, and his mother died when he was seven. Soon after his mother's death he went to Oregon to live with relatives, and there, at the age of thirteen, he began to earn his own living by working in truck gardens. At the same time he went to night school.

In 1891 Leland Stanford Junior University opened at Palo Alto, California, and Herbert Hoover was a freshman in the first class. He worked to pay his own way through the University, and was graduated as an engineer in 1895.

Work in many lands. Then an interesting life opened up for Hoover in many lands. He was a mining engineer. For a few years he worked for the United States government in California, Colorado, and New Mexico. Then he worked in Australia, in China, and in India.

Work in the World War. When the World War began in 1914, Mr. Hoover was in London. As the German armies marched into Belgium people were driven from their homes and began to suffer much for want of food and clothes.

Mr. Hoover saw that something must be done to prevent thousands of women and children from dying of starvation. He organized a group of helpers and appealed to people all over the world for gifts of money and goods to help the Belgians.

As the War went on, the work increased, because more and more people in Belgium and France were made homeless by the War. He had several thousand helpers, many of them young American men and women who were traveling in Europe when the War began. At one time Mr. Hoover had two hundred ships carrying food, medicines, clothing, and other supplies to the suffering people of Europe. He and his helpers and those who gave money and food saved an untold number of lives in Belgium and France. Most of the money and supplies were furnished by our government and by our people.

When the United States joined the World War,

President Wilson appointed Mr. Hoover Food Administrator. Now his work was on both sides of the Atlantic. He came back to the United States and urged the people to raise more foodstuffs and to avoid waste, so that our own soldiers and the poor people in Europe might have enough to eat.

Boys and girls were asked to eat very little sugar and candy, so that there would be enough sugar for the soldiers' food. People were asked to eat cornbread instead of wheat bread, so that the army might have wheat flour. They ate meat only once a day or every other day, so that meat might go to the soldiers and to the unfortunate Belgian and French families who were driven from their homes. Americans cheerfully saved and went without, and called it "Hooverizing."

After the War was over, the work increased. Many, many families in Germany, Austria, Poland, and Russia were almost starving. Little children, especially, were suffering. So Mr. Hoover carried on the relief work in those countries, getting money and goods from the more fortunate people in the United States, England, and other countries.

His work for the government. When the time came for the election of a new President in 1920, a great many people wanted to make Mr. Hoover President. He said that he favored the Republican party, but the Republican leaders were not ready to support him. Senator Warren G. Harding, of Ohio, was elected.

President Harding appointed Mr. Hoover to be Secretary of Commerce and one of the President's group of advisers. After President Harding's death, Mr.

Hoover continued to serve in this office under President Coolidge, and did much important work. In 1927 there was a terrible flood in the Mississippi River Valley. President Coolidge sent Mr. Hoover to help in the relief work and to study ways of preventing such floods in the future. Congress voted a large sum of money for this purpose. The plans for the work were drawn up by government engineers and began to be carried out in 1928.

The presidency. In 1928, Mr. Hoover was elected President. In the fall of 1929 a great industrial depression set in. Many banks failed and their depositors lost their money. People who were unable to pay taxes or rent lost their homes and farms. Factories and shops were closed, and workers were thrown out of work. When their savings were gone, many had to be helped by neighbors, welfare societies, community funds, and appropriations from taxes.

President Hoover tried to stop the tide of the depression. He opposed all inflation, or increase of the currency by the issue of paper money. Congress created the Reconstruction Finance Corporation, providing large sums of money for loans to banks, railroads, and other corporations to keep them going. A Home Loan Bank bill was also passed to provide loans to home owners so that they might not lose their homes.

A SHORT STORY TO TELL

There are two large political parties in the United States, the Republican party and the Democratic party. Each party tries to elect its own members to run the government. The Republicans have been the more successful. Since the death of President Lincoln the Democrats have won but five elections.

This chapter tells the story of two Democratic Presidents, Grover Cleveland and Woodrow Wilson, and of two Republican Presidents, Theodore Roosevelt and Herbert Hoover.

These Presidents tried, while they were in office, to govern the country for the benefit of all the people. They persuaded Congress to pass many good laws. They also tried to enforce the laws, and to make everybody obey them. They wanted everybody to have what we call a square deal.

President Roosevelt did much to save the forests and streams from being destroyed or misused. With his advice Congress set aside much of the government lands for parks, so that all the people can enjoy their beauty.

While Woodrow Wilson was President the United States entered the World War against Germany. When the war was over, he tried to get all Germany's enemies to make a fair peace. He did much for the farmers and the working people of the United States.

Herbert Hoover, the fourth of the leaders described in this chapter, became famous all over the world by his management of relief work among the suffering people of Belgium and France during the World War. When the United States went into the war, he entered the service of the government and remained in that service most of the time for the next twelve years. On March 4, 1929, he became President of the United States and served until 1933.

STORY HOUR

1. Divide the class into four groups. Let each group choose one of the four presidents presented in this chapter. The members of the group are to give a story about the president they have chosen. Each pupil is to do his share in telling the story. Vote to see which group was thought to be the best story-telling group.

NEW WORDS TO UNDERSTAND

2. Use the words below in written sentences that tell something about the four leaders in government.

Republicans	pensions
Democrats	Venezuela
political parties	conservation
presidency	riots
candidate	submarine
veto	irrigate
depression	currency

3. Read *Roosevelt's Letters to His Children*. It is one of the books you will enjoy in the list on page 230.

TRAVELING BY WATER

4. In a geography find a map of the Western Hemisphere (North and South America). Copy it, locating on your copy the Panama Canal. Show on it the shortest water route from Buenos Aires to San Francisco; from New York to Seattle; from London to San Francisco.

Chapter XVII

MARK TWAIN: THE "KING" OF AMERICAN WRITERS

Mark Twain.

Boyhood. In the preceding chapter, we read the story of Grover Cleveland. About a year and a half before Cleveland was born in the little New Jersey village where his father was preaching, another boy was born in the far-away state of Missouri. The name of this boy was Samuel L. Clemens, but we know him better as Mark Twain, a name that he gave himself after he was grown.

Mark Twain became the most famous American of his time. He was nearly as well known in Europe as he was in America. All over the world people laughed and cried over the books that he wrote, and he was known and loved wherever his books were read.

When Mark Twain was four years old his father moved to Hannibal, Missouri, a sleepy little town on the bank of the Mississippi River. Here, with other boys of his age, he learned to fish and hunt, to swim in the great river, to hike and camp, and to do the other things that boy scouts now do. The boys had a robbers' cave and many were the things they hid in it. But their greatest interest was to watch the steamboats puffing up and down the river and sometimes stopping at the village wharf to unload or take on freight. They thought the steamboat captains and the pilots the most important men in the world.

Going to work. At the age of twelve Mark Twain went to work in his brother's newspaper office. He did not go to school again, but in the printing office he learned to set type, he learned to write good English, and at home he read a great many books. For six years he really went to school in the newspaper office. He probably gave himself a better education there than most boys have when they leave the high school.

After leaving his brother's paper, Mark Twain worked on newspapers in Philadelphia and New York. Then he returned to Missouri and learned to be a steamboat pilot on the Mississippi River. He thought this the most interesting work that he would ever have a chance to do.

He traveled up and down the great river for nearly five years, and learned to know it as well as you know your own front yard. He had to know the deep and the shallow places, the currents, the sandbars, and the sunken logs and snags so that he could steer the boat safely. Many years later he wrote a book, *Life on the Mississippi*. It tells the story of his steamboat days.

How Mark Twain got his name. Sometimes it was necessary to measure the depth of the water. One of the workmen on the boat would drop a line overboard weighted with a piece of lead and would call out the depth to the pilot. There was a mark on the line six feet from the lead and another at twelve. When the water was six feet deep, the linesman would call, "mark one." When it was twelve feet deep, he would shout, "mark twain," meaning "mark two." When the pilot heard this shout, he knew that all was safe.

Later the young river pilot began to write stories for the newspapers and sign them "Mark Twain." This pen name became so popular that he continued to use it on his books. Many people thought it was his real name.

In the West. During the War between the North and the South most of the passenger boats quit running on the Mississippi and Mark Twain had to find another job. He went West—first to Nevada and later to California. He worked in the mines but could never find enough gold to keep him in spending money. Then he turned to writing stories for newspapers and magazines.

A funny story that he wrote about a jumping frog made him famous. Dozens of papers printed the story and all over the United States people laughed and talked about the jumping frog. It was the beginning of Mark Twain's career as a writer. He had found his life's work.

Tom and his friends come to their own funeral

His travels. While he was in the West Mark Twain made a trip to the Sandwich Islands. When he returned he went to New York, and the next year he sailed on a voyage to the Holy Land. Later he made many voyages to Europe. He lived for a while in Italy and spent much time in England and France. But Connecticut became his home. He built a beautiful mansion at Redding, Connecticut, which he called "Stormfield," and there he spent his later years.

His books. Mark Twain wrote a great many books. As we have already seen, he wrote a book about his steamboating days on the Mississippi. Another, called *Roughing It,* tells about his life in the West. *Innocents Abroad* tells the story of his trip to the Holy Land. In fact, he wrote a book about nearly every long tour that he ever took.

He loved children, especially boys, and liked to write for them. *Tom Sawyer* and *Huckleberry Finn* are stories of his own boyhood and of the boys with whom he played on the banks of the Mississippi. Many people think them the best books ever written for boys. *The Prince and the Pauper* is a delightful story of how a young prince of England changed places with a poor boy of London. The prince played the poor boy for a while and the poor boy lived the life of the prince. Both found much to amuse them in the change, but the poor boy learned that the life of the prince was not filled with pleasures and play. He saw that the prince had to work hard in order to learn to be a good king.

The book that Mark Twain liked best was his *Personal Recollections of Joan of Arc,* the peasant girl who led the French armies against the English and saved the French nation. He said that he studied many years to be able to write the book, and it took him two years to finish it after he began to write it.

Boys and girls loved Mark Twain almost as much as he loved them. A magazine for children once offered a prize for the best cartoon or funny picture of a well-known man. A few pictures of congressmen, politicians, and rich men were sent in, but the cartoons of Mark Twain filled a wheelbarrow. When the editor of the magazine told him about it, he wrote: "No tribute could have pleased me more than that—the friendship of the children."

University honors. Mark Twain never studied in a college or university. He did not even go to school after he was twelve years old. But three great universities honored him with their diplomas. Yale University made him doctor of literature. The University of Missouri made him doctor of laws.

But the honor that he probably valued more than anything else that ever happened to him was the degree of doctor of letters from the University of Oxford, the oldest university in England. The King and Queen entertained him. The Lord Mayor of London gave him a banquet. All the leading writers in England welcomed him and praised his books. A London paper declared that his books and his visit had done more to strengthen the friendship between the United States and England than anything else that had ever happened.

The "King" of American literature. Mark Twain died in 1910. He was seventy-five years old. A few years before his death his friends gave him a birthday dinner. There were nearly two hundred people at the dinner, most of them writers. They called Mark Twain the "King of American writers." They rightly regarded him as the greatest American writer of his day. He was one of the great men of the world.

A SHORT STORY TO TELL

Mark Twain was the greatest American humorist, and perhaps he was the greatest writer that our nation has yet produced. Other writers of his time loved and admired him and called him the King.

When a boy Mark Twain worked in a printing office. Perhaps it was here that he learned to write so well. He did not go to school after he was twelve years old.

Mark Twain had a busy and interesting life. He learned to be a pilot on a steamboat running up and down the Mississippi River. He crossed the plains to California in a stage coach and tried his luck in the gold mines. He was a newspaper writer and traveled extensively in Europe and other parts of the world.

Nearly everything that Mark Twain saw or did gave him an idea for a book or a story. He wrote books about his boyhood friends, about his steamboat days, about his trip to the West, and about his trips to Europe. His best books for children are *Tom Sawyer, Huckleberry Finn,* and *The Prince and the Pauper.*

UNDERSTANDING MARK TWAIN

1. Make a list of the things that made people like Mark Twain.

2. Why does the name, "King" of American writers, seem to be a good title for Mark Twain?

3. Bring to class some further information about Mark Twain that you have found in other books.

4. Have you read any of Mark Twain's books? If so tell something that amused you in one of the stories.

DO YOU KNOW THE ANSWER?

5. What is a humorist?
6. What is a river pilot?
7. What is a pen name?
8. What does "mark twain" mean?
9. What is a tour?

Chapter XVIII

SAMUEL GOMPERS: THE GREATEST AMERICAN LABOR LEADER

Samuel Gompers

Life in London. Samuel Gompers, the great leader of American working people, was born in London in 1850. He died in San Antonio, Texas, in 1924.

Just a little while before his death Mr. Gompers finished writing the story of his life, and we can read about his childhood in his own words. "The first home that I remember," he wrote; "was in a three-story brick house at No. 2 Fort Street, in East Side, London. Like all the other houses in the neighborhood, ours had worn gray with the passing years.

"My father and mother lived on the ground floor. My grandparents lived in the second story with their four girls and a boy, who was ten months older than I

"Our apartment consisted of one large front room and a little back room which we used for storage and for things which had to be kept cool. In the summertime father built bunks in the little room and we children slept there. In the winter-time we all slept in the big room—Father and Mother in the big bed that had a curtain around it, and we children in a trundle bed that was rolled under the big bed in the daytime.

"I was the oldest. Besides me there were Henry, Alexander, Lewis, and Jack. That front room was sitting-room, bedroom, dining-room, and kitchen."

The father was a cigar-maker. Though the family was very poor, there was always enough to eat, the room was scrubbed and clean, and the children were happy. When he was an old man Samuel still remembered the delicious dinners that his mother cooked in the open fireplace.

They bought their bread at the bakery. "I was always glad to be sent to purchase the loaf," said Samuel. "We bought a four-pound loaf. If the big round loaf was a bit under weight, an extra slice was cut from another loaf. That extra slice never reached home."

Education. When he was six years old the little boy started to school. He went to the Jewish Free School and studied reading, writing, arithmetic, and history. As he grew older he studied French, music, and Hebrew. His mother and father had lived in Holland until they were grown and they sometimes spoke Dutch. He learned the Dutch language from them. Later he learned also to read and speak German.

At the age of ten the little boy had to leave school

and go to work. At first he started to learn the shoe-
maker's trade. His wages were six cents a week. But
he did not like shoemaking, so his father allowed him
to learn cigar-making. He liked this work and in
three or four years he became a skillful workman.

In the shop he heard a lot about America. The war
between the North and the South was going on and
everybody was talking about the "land of the free."
He learned a song that caused him to want to go there:

"To the west, to the west, to the land of the free
Where mighty Missouri rolls down to the sea,
Where a man is a man if he's willing to toil,
And the humblest may gather the fruits of the soil.
Away! far away, let us hope for the best
And build up a home in the land of the west."

Family move to New York. In 1863 the Gompers
family moved to New York. Samuel was thirteen and
a half years old. For a little while he helped his father
make cigars at home, but the next year, when he was
fourteen, he got a job in a factory. From that time
to the end of his life, sixty years later, he did a man's
work. He worked in the factory all day, but at night
he went to school, attended lectures, and often took part
in a debating club. He was determined to be an educated man.

In 1864 the fourteen year old boy joined the Cigar
Makers' Union. That was really the beginning of his
life work. He continued for many years to make
cigars, but he began to study about plans to make the
working people more happy and comfortable. He had

lived among workmen all his life and he knew how poor and miserable they sometimes were both in England and in the United States.

Devotes life to labor unions. Gompers saw that the working people who were doing different kinds of work must unite and help one another. By acting together, he thought that they could get many things that they needed. They might get their employers to provide safer and more comfortable places in which to work, and pay better wages. They might get Congress and state legislatures to pass laws reducing the number of hours that men and women had to work each day.

So Samuel Gompers set to work to try to get all the different classes of workers into a union. In 1886 he started the big union that is known as the American Federation of Labor. He was president of this big union of workers for thirty-seven years.

During those thirty-seven years the condition of the working people changed very greatly not only in the United States but all over the world. Factories and offices and stores made working conditions more comfortable and healthful for both men and women. The working day was reduced to eight hours, and many workmen got a half holiday on Saturday. Wages were increased so that workmen could send their children to school and give their families comfortable homes. The American Federation of Labor helped to bring these changes about.

Mr. Gompers was happy to see the condition of the working people so much improved, but he was never satisfied. He kept on working. He tried to help the workmen of other countries as well as those of the United States. Just a little while before his death he wrote: "I hope to keep on with my work until I go out into the silence."

He had his wish. When he died he was returning to his home in Washington. He had been to Mexico to help the poor people of that foreign country.

Millions of people are happier and more comfortable today because of what Samuel Gompers did to improve the conditions under which they work.

A SHORT STORY TO TELL

Samuel Gompers spent most of his life working to improve the lives of laboring people. He was born in London, and his father and mother were very poor. He had four brothers. Although the family was very poor, he used to say that the boys had a good time and were happy.

His parents moved to America when he was thirteen years old. He learned to be a cigar-maker and worked at that trade for many years.

He saw that the working people had very hard lives. They worked long hours and got very little pay. Some of them worked in dirty, uncomfortable, and unhealthful places. He began to wonder how their working conditions could be improved. It occurred to him that all the working people ought to unite and take part in making agreements with their employers.

So he organized the American Federation of Labor. He was president of this big union for thirty-seven years. All of the workers did not join it, but it did a great deal to help make the working people of the United States happier and more comfortable than the workers in any other country.

MORE ABOUT LABOR UNIONS

1. What is a labor union?

2. What is the A. F. of L.?

3. Find out how many of the fathers of the pupils in your class belong to labor unions or employ men who belong to unions. List the names of these unions to see whether or not there are many different unions represented.

4. Perhaps you can find out who took Gompers' place as president of the American Federation of Labor. Who is the president today?

5. Try to find out some of the things that labor unions are working for today.

Chapter XIX

LUTHER BURBANK, WHO
CREATED NEW PLANTS

Why Burbank is in history. Any man who does something to change the life of a great many people helps to make history. We study Edison because he gave us the electric light, which illuminates our homes and our streets. Mark Twain wrote books that give pleasure to millions of people. Alexander Graham Bell invented the telephone, which adds so much to our convenience and our enjoyment of life. Henry Ford made an automobile so inexpensive that it gave pleasure and service to people all over the world. These men who invented machines and did important things deserve a place in our books. We are constantly reminded of them by the things we see around us.

Luther Burbank also made things. He made new trees, new and better fruit, more beautiful and more fragrant flowers. If Burbank could have put his name on what he made, or improved, as other men have done, then we might see his name on the potatoes, plums, prunes, dewberries, and pears that come to our table. When we go into the garden we should see it on the Shasta daisy, the larkspur, the star flower, the rose, and spineless cactus. Even the odor of the dahlia and the fragrance of the verbena would bear his name.

Burbank added millions of dollars to the wealth of the world, yet he gathered for himself little of that wealth. His purpose was to give rather than to take. By improving plants, he gave food; by creating more beautiful flowers, he helped to beautify the world.

Boyhood in Massachusetts. Luther Burbank was born in 1849 in a small town near Boston. He early showed a love for books, for flowers, and for all kinds of plant life. As a child he played with flowers, as most children do with animals and mechanical toys. Flowers were his pets. Some one gave him a potted cactus plant, which he often carried around with him. One day he fell and broke the pot and ruined the plant. He grieved over it as most boys would grieve over the death of a pet dog.

As a boy, Luther Burbank was very poor. At an early age he went to work in a factory at fifty cents a day. It was not enough to pay his living expenses. Finally he left the factory and began work as a gardener. This gave him an opportunity to study the plant-life he loved so well.

One day Burbank noticed a seed-ball on top of a potato stalk. He watched it from day to day, for such seed-balls are not common. One day when he came into the garden it was gone. Burbank was in despair. But he found it on the ground. He planted the seeds and from one of the potatoes which grew from this planting came the famous Burbank potato. Its use has spread all over the world, and it furnishes food yearly to millions of people.

Goes to California. When a young man Burbank moved to California. His early years in California were hard. Once he had a job cleaning chicken coops, and at night he slept in one of the coops. When work failed, he was in want. After a time he got a job in a nursery, but his pay was so small that he had to sleep over the steaming hothouse.

Because of these conditions, the young gardener's health gave way, and he came down with fever. Wan and haggard, he rose from his sick bed and began anew the search for work. As soon as he was able he bought a small nursery.

The beginning of his life work. Then one day the opportunity of Burbank's life came, as it often does to people of such courage and industry. A man ordered twenty thousand prune trees, to be delivered in nine months. It really did not seem to be a great opportunity, but Burbank made the most of it.

The young nursery-man had no prune trees and it would require two and a half years to grow them. He knew that the only tree that would grow rapidly enough to meet the need was the almond. So he planted more than twenty thousand almonds and nursed the little trees along as fast as he could. Then he took buds from prune trees and grafted them on the almond stems. At the end of nine months he delivered twenty thousand prune trees, which grew into one of the finest prune orchards of California.

Creating new forms of plant life. After a time, Burbank sold his nursery and decided to devote all his time to improving plant life. He did this in three quite different ways.

First, he improved certain old varieties of fruits, flowers, and vegetables by selecting the best of a kind and planting the seed. This he did over and over again until he got a desired result.

Second, he crossed-fertilized plants which bore good fruit with wild ones which had stronger roots. He did this by sprinkling the pollen from one plant into the flower-cup of another. The result was a new plant having the strength of the wild root and the fine fruit of the garden plant. Often this cross fertilizing was done to change the size, the color, or the odor of a flower; or the size, color, flavor, or keeping quality of a fruit.

Third, he created new forms of plant life by watching the plants and selecting the strange new forms which sometimes appear as if by a freak of nature. He carefully cultivated these freak plants, called "sports," and planted the seeds of the best. When the new plants grew, he again selected and planted the seeds of the best. By repeating this process several times he would get the sort of plant that he wanted.

The story of the walnut trees. In front of the Burbank home in California is a row of noble wide-spread-
ing walnut trees, which bear the finest nuts. They
have an interesting history. Burbank started with a
common English walnut and a California black walnut. By sprinkling the center of the flower of one tree
with the pollen from the blossoms of the other, he got
a new sort of nut. He planted this, and, when it grew
into a tree and bore nuts, he again selected and planted
the best. After selecting and planting the best nuts
several times, he developed a tree that satisfied him.
He called it the *Paradox*.

A half-dozen of these trees were set out and left to
themselves. In fourteen years they had grown to a
height of eighty feet, with a top-spread of seventy-
five feet, and a trunk two feet in diameter. The wood
is hard, takes a good polish for furniture, and makes
fine fuel. Nearby are some of the old, unimproved
trees. They are more than twice as old as the Paradox
walnuts, but they are only twenty feet high, and eight
inches in diameter.

The Shasta daisy. Burbank found in California a
small field daisy. The plant grew everywhere, and
was considered a pest. It overran farms and lawns,
and everybody hated it. Burbank decided to give it a
better place in the world. In England he found a
larger and coarser daisy than his wild California
friend, and in Japan he found a third, possessing a
dazzling whiteness. He brought the three together,
just as he had the two walnuts, and created the largest
and most beautiful daisy that we know.

A man who found his work.

The Shasta daisy has the hardihood of the California daisy, and the beauty of the Japanese variety. It will grow anywhere, from the snow line to the equator, and the cut-flowers will remain fresh and beautiful in water for a long time.

The spineless cactus. Those who have lived or traveled in the West and Southwest know that much of the country is overgrown with thorny cactus. Some of the land is so dry that it will grow little except cactus and sage brush. The cactus stores up in its leaves a large amount of water, and furnishes both food and drink for cattle. The only trouble is that the cattle can hardly eat the plant on account of the thorns. Ranchmen often burn off the thorns and then feed the juicy leaves to the hungry cattle.

Burbank thought he could benefit mankind, and animals too, by producing a cactus without thorns. He selected a plant with the fewest thorns and planted the seeds. When the new plants grew, he again selected the seeds from the least thorny plants. After repeating this process many times, he finally produced what is known as the spineless or thornless cactus. In this way he made the dry lands more useful and productive than they had been before.

Other wonders. All of the many things that Burbank has led plants to do can not be told here. A man who wrote the life of this plant wizard has described him as the man who gave plants what they most desired. Let us imagine that one flower with a strong stem and a small and homely blossom wanted beauty more than anything else. Burbank developed it until it stood forth in radiant beauty. Another did not like its color. Burbank changed it from golden to red. The dahlia had beauty but a wretched odor. Burbank studied it for twenty-five years, and finally not only drove from it the offensive odor, but gave it the fragrance of the magnolia.

What Burbank means to the world. In olden times, if a man had done the things that Burbank did with plants, he would have been accused of being a magician. Perhaps he would have been put to death. But we know that there was no magic about his work. He had merely studied the life of plants, and helped nature make the changes. His work has increased the world's food supply. It has made the desert more productive. It has created millions of dollars' worth of flowers, fruits, and trees.

Burbank said of himself: "I love sunshine, the blue sky, trees, flowers, mountains, green meadows, running brooks, the ocean when its waves softly ripple along the sandy beach or when pounding the rocky cliffs with its thunder and roar, the birds of the field, the waterfalls, the rainbow, the dawn, the noonday, and the evening sunset,—but children above them all."*

Surely we must count Luther Burbank as one of the most useful men that our country has produced. He did what he wanted to do. He made the world a better and more beautiful place than he found it.

*From W. S. Harwood, *New Creations in Plant Life,* By permission of the Macmillan Company.

A SHORT STORY TO TELL

Luther Burbank has a place in history because he improved many kinds of plants. All his life he was interested in plants, and from childhood to old age he made a close study of them. His early days in Massachusetts were filled with poverty and distress, but always he held to one purpose, the improvement and development of plants. He went to California in 1875 and became a gardener, later a nurseryman, and later still he gave up the nursery and devoted all his time to improving plants, and to creating new kinds.

This wonderful naturalist made prunes grow on almond trees by grafting; he produced the great Paradox walnut by crossing; he developed and named the Shasta daisy; he made cactus grow without thorns; and, after twenty-five years of labor, he succeeded in ridding the dahlia of a bad odor and giving it the fragrance of a magnolia blossom.

The results of Burbank's study and patient work added millions of dollars to the wealth of the world and made life more beautiful for us all.

THINGS TO DO

1. In encyclopedias find out all you can about grafting trees.

2. Explain why Burbank was called the "Plant Wizard."

3. Perhaps you can find the names of other plants that were improved or discovered by Burbank. Have as long a list as possible.

Chapter XX

SOME WOMEN LEADERS IN THE MAKING OF OUR NATION

Then.   Now.

THE OLD IDEA OF WOMEN'S WORK

Pioneers and home-makers. The old idea was that women should stay at home, keep the house, attend to the children, do the family sewing, nurse the sick, and then, if a little time was left, work the garden and look after the chickens. Both men and women thought that it would be wrong for women to take part in business or to have any share in running the government.

In colonial times, as we have seen, the girls did not even go to the same schools that the boys attended, and at church the women sat on one side of the room and

(277)

the men on the other. People had a strange sort of feeling that women were much better than men, and yet not so good.

In the beginning of our country women worked side by side with their men. They went with the pioneers into the forests. They crossed the mountains with the men and did their part in building homes on the banks of the Mississippi. Later they crossed the plains in "covered wagons" and settled new homes on the shores of the Pacific.

Women shared all the dangers of the men and most of their labors. They worked in the little fields, planting corn and potatoes and peas; and with rifle in hand they guarded their lonely cabins in the woods in the absence of the men.

In spite of danger, hard work, and suffering, women were denied most of the privileges that men enjoyed. Married women could not manage their own property. It belonged to their husbands.

Women could not go to college and learn to be doctors and lawyers and teachers. They could not hold public offices and help make the laws. They could not even vote for public officers and help carry out the laws.

The men did not mean to be unfair to women. Most of them honestly believed that women were too good and pure to take part in voting and running the government. They knew that women made the best nurses, but they thought them unfit for the work of a doctor.

A doctor had to make visits in all sorts of weather

and at all hours of the day and night. They said that women were not strong enough to do such work.

A lawyer had to go into court and try cases. He had to mix in the quarrels of men and hear about the evil doings of law-breakers and criminals. Therefore they thought women too good for the work of a lawyer.

THE OLD IDEA OF WOMEN CHANGES

Women want the privileges of men. Very slowly the old idea changed. Some of the women began to say that, since they helped do all of the hard things that men did, they wanted also to share the privileges of the men. They wanted to go to college. They wanted to learn to be doctors and lawyers and preachers and teachers. They wanted to vote, and they wanted to hold office and help make the laws and manage the government.

Women go to work outside the home. When cotton and woolen factories began to be built about a hundred years ago, women went to work in them. Going out to the factories, where they stayed from sunrise until dark, was the first step which took women out of the home. Their work became more like the work of the men. One could no longer say that "woman's work is in the home."

As more factories were built, more and more women went into them. Later they began to work in some kinds of stores and in offices.

Women go to college. Toward the middle of the nineteenth century colleges and universities in the western states began to open their doors to women and teach them the same subjects that were taught to the men. Oberlin College in Ohio was the first to teach men and women in the same classes. Other colleges in the Mississippi Valley quickly followed the example.

New York has the honor of starting the first colleges for women in the old eastern states. Elmira College was opened in 1855. A few years later Mathew Vassar gave the money to start Vassar College at Poughkeepsie, New York. He believed that women ought to have a college as good as any for men. Soon other colleges for women were built, and most of the old colleges opened their doors to women.

Women did much of the work in the early New England factory.

Working in a textile mill.

THE RIGHT TO VOTE AND HOLD OFFICE

Women long denied the right to vote. Women became teachers in the public schools and carried on much of the school's share in education. They became doctors and lawyers, and some of them became preachers. They went to work in offices as stenographers and bookkeepers. They managed stores and worked on newspapers. They did all of the things that men could do except one thing—they did not vote. The laws did not allow them to vote.

The long struggle for the vote. Two New York women, Susan B. Anthony and Elizabeth Cady Stanton, took the lead in winning for women the right to vote. They worked constantly, and at first their efforts did not have great results, but they never gave up.

Miss Anthony lived to be a very old woman. She was eighty-six years old when she died. She never married. She did not have a house to keep or children to take care of, so she was always free to carry on her work for women.

Once Miss Anthony declared that she knew she had the right to vote, so she went to the voting place and voted. An officer arrested her and took her into court for voting contrary to the law. The judge fined her a hundred dollars, but she declared that she would never pay the fine, and she never did.

She traveled in many states, and everywhere she went she made speeches, trying to show the people that women ought to have the same rights as men.

Mrs. Stanton was married and had a husband and children to look after. She could not travel as much as Miss Anthony but she could stay at home and write. She and Miss Anthony started a magazine and called it *The Revolution*. They published in it letters and arguments and speeches about the right of women to vote and hold office.

People laughed and made fun of these earnest women, but they kept right on with their work. Nothing could stop them, they said, until the laws gave them the right to vote.

The women gain the right to vote. By 1900 four states allowed women to vote on the same terms as men. Wyoming took the lead in 1890. Colorado, Idaho, and

Utah followed. By 1914 seven other western states had granted full voting rights to women. These seven states were Washington, California, Arizona, Kansas, Oregon, Montana, and Nevada. Now there were eleven states in which women could vote.

President Roosevelt was the first President who made any special effort to try to help women get the right to vote.

During the World War President Wilson took up the fight for women, and finally the Constitution of the United States was changed, or amended, in such a way as to give women the right to vote in all the states.

Women can now vote in all of the states; and in many of the states, as well as in the national government, they can hold office the same as men. Nowadays there are women members of Congress, and many women are serving acceptably in various kinds of public office.

Women's work in the government. But women did not have to wait for the right to vote in order to do important things in the government. We have already seen how our government protects the welfare of the people by wise laws, how it looks after the health and education of the people. Women have had much to do with the passing of such laws. To tell the whole story of what women have done for the welfare and happiness of the American people would take a large volume. We can study here but one thing more. We must learn how a woman started the American Red Cross Society.

Women now do much more office work than men.

CLARA BARTON AND THE AMERICAN RED CROSS

Miss Barton's early years. Clara Barton grew up on a farm in Massachusetts. She had two brothers and two sisters. Being the baby of the family, she was petted and spoiled. She liked to do things her own way and was sometimes hard to get on with. She was timid among people, but she was brave enough to ride the colts on the farm and to cross streams on floating logs.

When fifteen years old, Miss Barton began to teach school, and she was a fine teacher. When she was older she went to New Jersey. Schools were not free schools in those days, and Miss Barton saw a great many children playing in the streets. Their parents could not pay to send them to school. She told the school trustees that she would teach three months without pay, if they would make the school free and take in all the children. They agreed to do it, and before long there were so many children in school that they needed a larger building.

Her war work. Miss Barton was forty years old when the war began between the North and the South. She heard dreadful stories about the suffering of soldiers wounded in battle.

Miss Barton determined to make things easier for the sick and wounded men. She put an advertisement in the newspapers asking for supplies for the soldiers. She promised to see that the things got to the men who needed help, if the people would send them to her. Supplies came pouring in and she sent them on to the places where they were most needed.

After she had been carrying on this sort of work for about a year the army commanders gave her a pass and allowed her to go wherever she pleased for the purpose of nursing the sick and wounded and supplying them with food and clothing.

Though Miss Barton's work was with the Union armies, it made no difference to her whether a wounded man was from the North or the South. She helped all who were sick and suffering.

Her work in Europe. Five years after the War between the North and the South ended Miss Barton was in Europe. A war was going on between Germany and France, and she plunged into the work of helping the sick and wounded, just as she had done in her own country. She worked both in France and in Germany.

She starts the American Red Cross Society. In Europe Miss Barton learned about the work of the Red Cross Society, which had been organized to do relief work among sick and wounded soldiers.

Miss Barton wanted to start an American branch of the society. Before she could get the American branch to work with the European society, our government would have to sign a treaty with European countries, saying how the Red Cross Society should carry on its work in time of war. Finally Miss Barton got what she wanted. The United States signed the treaty, and the American Red Cross was started.

Then Miss Barton got the Red Cross to do all sorts of relief work in peace time. The Red Cross workers now nurse, feed, and help sufferers from storms, floods, fires, and disease. And when there is a war they do all they can to help the wounded men on each side and to feed and clothe the poor families of the soldiers.

In 1905 the American branch took the name of the National Red Cross Society. The President of the United States is its president, and the War Department has some control over its money.

JANE ADDAMS AND HULL HOUSE

Jane Addams' early life. Jane Addams was born in Cedarville, Illinois, a small town a little more than one hundred miles west of Chicago. Her father was a miller. On one of her trips to the Freeport mills with her father she saw for the first time the way in which poor people lived. She was so sad over the poorly clothed, dirty, children that she said to her father, "When I'm a grown-up lady, I want to live right next door to poor people, and the children can play in my yard."

As a young woman Jane Addams visited the slums, or poor districts, of London. Again the suffering of the people made her wish to do something for them.

Hull House is bought. In 1889 when Jane Addams returned from Europe she went to Chicago with her friend Ellen Starr. They bought a house in a very poor district. The house had once belonged to a wealthy man named Charles Hull and was still called "Hull House."

Here Miss Addams and Miss Starr lived and became real neighbors to the poor people around them. All were welcome who came to Hull House. Many came again and again to the classes in cooking, sewing, and weaving, to the clubs and meetings held in the big house. Jane Addams' wish to help the poor had come true.

A SHORT STORY TO TELL

Women worked side by side with the men in the making of the United States. They suffered hardships and risked their lives among the Indians just as the men did. But for a long, long time they were not allowed to go to college; they were not allowed to enter the professions; and they could take no part in the management of the government.

At last women began to say that they ought to have

the same rights that men had, and they demanded the right to vote. Miss Susan B. Anthony and Mrs. Elizabeth Cady Stanton took the lead in the struggle for the vote.

The western states were the first to give women the right to vote. President Roosevelt and President Wilson asked Congress to help change the government so that women could vote in all the states. Finally the change was made in 1920.

Women did not need the vote to do important things in our country, but it was fair and right for them to have the privilege of voting just as the men did.

One of the most important things ever done by a woman in our country was the starting of the American Red Cross Society. Miss Clara Barton has the credit for doing that fine work.

Jane Addams began the Settlement at Hull House to offer friendship and help to the poor in the slums of Chicago. Since then many settlements have been started to bring cheer and aid to the poor of our great cities.

HELPING OTHERS

1. Prepare a report on the work of the Red Cross. You might do this in the form of a pageant.

2. Perhaps your class belongs to the Junior Red Cross. Have a number of talks given in which the work of the Junior Red Cross is explained.

3. Find out about the work done in settlement houses. Find out why there is a need for such places.

4. Tell the story of the struggle that women had before they were given the right to vote.

UNIT SEVEN

THE LAND THAT WE LIVE IN

When we use our imaginations and try to visit the homes of our great great grand parents we can hardly believe that we live in the same world that they found so interesting.

Less than a hundred years ago the first railroads were being built. There were no automobiles or airplanes. There were no telegraph lines, telephones, or radios; no electric lights, no running water in houses, no modern refrigerators or furnaces.

Discoveries and inventions have changed all our ways of living. Lindbergh flies across the ocean alone. Byrd goes to the North Pole and the South Pole in an airplane, and talks and sends messages over his radio ten thousand miles away as if he were in the next county.

There were no large cities in those olden times. Now more than half of our people live in cities and towns. The rise of cities has caused our governments to give more attention to the pleasure and entertainment of their inhabitants. We have city, county, state, and national parks; and much money is spent in encouraging and teaching children and grown people to play games of various kinds.

The possessions of the United States have spread to Alaska, the Hawaiian Islands, Puerto Rico, and the Isthmus of Panama; while, for nearly forty years it ruled the Philippine Islands. Our business men have interests in all parts of the world. A war in Europe or in China endangers the safety and welfare of our people. Inventions, discoveries and machinery have brought all the peoples of the world close together.

It is a beautiful and wonderful world that we live in. Our ancestors helped to make it what it is. They solved their problems and did their duty for us. Shall we solve our problems as well and do our duty to those who follow us? That is a question that your school must help to answer.

STORIES TO READ FOR UNIT SEVEN

Dalgliesh, Alice, *America Travels; the Story of a Hundred Years of Travel in America* (The Macmillan Company).

Hader, Mrs. B., and Hader, Elmer, *Picture Book of Travel* (The Macmillan Company).

Lent, H. B., *Wide Road Ahead! The Building of an Automobile* (The Macmillan Company).

Floherty, J. J., *Board the Airlines* (Doubleday, Doran and Company).

Webster, H. H., *World's Messengers* (Houghton, Mifflin Company).

Yard, R. S., *National Park Portfolio* (Superintendent of Documents).

O'Brien, J. S., *By Dog Sled With Byrd* (The Follett Publishing Company).

Chapter XXI

THE MAGIC EFFECTS OF MACHINERY

Alexander Graham Bell.

A STORY OF AMAZING PROGRESS

Increase in the number of people. Since the war between the North and the South, the people in the United States have increased from thirty-five million to nearly a hundred and thirty million. These hundred and thirty million people enjoy comforts and pleasures not even dreamed of by their fathers and grandfathers only a few short years ago.

Improvements in ways of traveling and sending news. One reason for our comforts and pleasures is the ease, cheapness, and speed with which we can travel, ship goods, and send news.

(291)

Railroads cross the United States from east to west and from north to south like lines on a gridiron. Alongside the railroads there are paved roads, on which trucks, busses, and automobiles travel with the speed of express trains. Airplanes roar overhead, carrying mail and precious freight. Telegraph and telephone wires stretch mile after mile along the roads, carrying millions of messages every day. And radio waves fill the air and carry the human voice to places that telegrams and telephone calls cannot reach.

A nation of cities. The railroads, the automobiles, and the telegraph and telephone lines have helped to make the United States a nation of cities. More than half of our nearly hundred and thirty million people live in cities and towns.

And such grand and elegant cities! Paved streets, lighted by electricity! Buildings forty stories high and three stories below ground! Buildings with offices for ten thousand people! Hotels with rooms for five thousand people; a bathroom, hot and cold water, steam heat, telephone, electric lights, fans, and radio in every room!

Stores that cover a block and furnish work for thousands of workers! Shops and factories turning out goods for the whole world; making machinery, tools, clothing, household and kitchen furniture, and all the things that people need!

Parks, museums, libraries, and art galleries to amuse and teach the swarming millions of the cities! And schools of such size and comfort and beauty as would have made Benjamin Franklin and Thomas Jefferson speechless with wonder!

But great cities are not all comfort and happiness. In every big city there are parts that are dreary and sad. In wretched shacks, or in huge barn-like buildings crowded close together, whole families of five or six people live in one or two rooms. Children are half-starved and lack clothing to go out of doors. Because of poor living conditions, sickness is common and the care of a doctor or a nurse is rare. Books, music, pictures, and flowers are almost unknown. And yet, even in these things progress is being made. City governments, public welfare clubs, and social service workers are doing much to better unhappy conditions in the cities.

Improvements in rural life. The people in the country have changed as greatly in their ways of living as those in the cities. Many farm houses now have all the comforts of city homes. They have electric lights, bathrooms, furnace heat, ice, telephone, and radio; and the rural mail carrier brings the daily newspaper to the door.

By using tractors, cultivators, planters, and reapers, one man can do the work of a farm more easily than ten men could do it seventy years ago. The automobile carries to the city market the things raised on the farm, and takes the farmer's family to the "movies," to church, and to shop. The automobile, the good roads, the telephone, the radio, and the rural mail delivery and parcel post have really taken the country to the city and the city to the country.

But still, as in the cities, all is not comfort and happiness. Many people live in tumble-down cabins on rented land. There is much sickness caused by dirt and flies and mosquitoes. Many children are kept from school because they must work or because their parents cannot give them proper clothes.

Let us turn now to the history of some of the things which have made such marvelous changes in the lives of the American people.

TALKING AND SENDING MESSAGES BY ELECTRICITY

The telegraph. We have already had the story of the beginning of the telegraph. Very soon telegraph messages were going from New York to San Francisco, and across the ocean by cable to Europe. Now the wires on land and the cables under the seas bring all the countries of the world close together.

The telephone. The telephone, which carries the human voice over a wire, was invented in 1876 by Alexander Graham Bell, a teacher of speech in Boston University. This was four years after Morse, the inventor of telegraphy, died. Professor Bell was a Scotchman. He was educated in Scotland and England, but his studies and experiments that gave us the telephone were carried on in the United States.

It is said that the people of the United States use the telephone more than any other people in the world. Can you think of any reason why?

Wireless. In 1899 William Marconi, an Italian, invented a way to send messages through the air without the use of telegraph wires. It is known as "wireless telegraphy," or simply "wireless." This is another marvelous advance in long distance communication.

Radio. Along about 1925 the radio came into general use in the United States. The radio is a sort of wireless telephone. It enables people to hear speeches and music over great distances and it has come to be of great importance in carrying on business and education.

Changes made by rapid communication. We can notice here only a few of the useful changes that the telegraph, telephone, wireless, and radio have made in the way we live.

First, we can carry on business much more quickly than our grandfathers could. Business that it used to take weeks and months to settle when General Jackson was President can be settled now by two or three telegrams, or by a few minutes' talk over the telephone.

Second, life and property are safer than they would be without such inventions. We can give a fire alarm, call a doctor, a nurse, or a policeman by telephone. Ships in danger at sea can call other ships to their help by wireless.

Third, life is brighter and happier. We no longer lose touch with our loved ones when they are away. We can reach them in a few minutes with a telegram, or we can talk with them over the telephone. Even on the ocean we can get messages to them by wireless. By radio we can send messages and listen to concerts, speeches, and sermons a thousand miles away. All the people in the world have been drawn closer together by these wonderful inventions.

Electrical machines and inventions. None of our machines and inventions are more important than those which harness electricity and make it work for man.

Edison at work in his laboratory.

We have already talked of the telegraph and telephone, of wireless and the radio. They all require electricity. Our automobiles and gas engines, too, must have electricity to make them go. They stop when the battery quits working.

Edison, the wizard of electricity. Many inventors have helped to make electricity work for men, but none has done more than Thomas A. Edison. He made so many and such wonderful inventions that the newspapers nicknamed him "the wizard." Even Aladdin's magical lamp did no greater wonders for him than electricity did for Edison.

Edison was born in a little town in Ohio. When he was eleven years old he became a newsboy on a train, selling papers, fruit, and candy to the passengers. Then he learned to be a telegraph operator. He spent only a few months in school, but he was always a hard worker, reading and thinking and teaching himself.

The first important thing that he did was to make a better telegraph instrument. He made enough money from this invention to set up a laboratory and hire helpers. From that time on, one marvelous invention after another came out of his workshop to take its place in our homes.

The electric light is the greatest of his inventions. It is used in nearly every town house in the United States, and in the farthest parts of the world. It is used in India, in China, in Africa. It is used wherever men go with an automobile or an airplane, and it guides ships on the water or in the air.

Another of Edison's inventions, the phonograph, has increased people's pleasure and happiness beyond our power to measure or describe. People living on far western ranches, on southern farms, and in northern lumber camps can put a record on the machine and hear the greatest singers and musicians in the world. Just suppose the phonograph had been invented a hundred years earlier; we could today hear George Washington's voice.

When Edison was trying to solve a problem, he worked day and night, sleeping only a few hours and hardly taking time to eat. This went on sometimes for weeks and months. He could not rest until the job was done; and then he would soon start on a new problem. Edison died in 1931, just fifty years after he invented the electric light.

History tells us of but one Edison. We cannot do the things that Edison has done, but by working hard we can all add a great deal to our usefulness in the world.

LIVING BY MACHINERY

The machine age. We live in an age of machinery. In much of what we do from morning until night machinery has had a part.

We rise in the morning from beds made by machinery. All of the clothes that we put on were probably made by machinery. Our cereal and bacon are prepared and brought to us by machinery. The bread for our toast is probably mixed by machinery, and the wheat from which it is made is handled by machinery from the time it was planted until it is put on our table.

The morning paper is a product of machinery. The typesetting of our books, the printing and binding are done by machines. Probably every piece of furniture in our home is machine made. We ride to school or to work in some kind of machine, an automobile or electric street car. We sit at a desk made by machinery and write with a pen or pencil made by machinery, or with a typewriter which is itself a wonderful machine. Our marbles, tops, balls, bats, gloves, skates—everything with which we play—are made by machinery.

The inventions and discoveries of men. All these changes have been brought about through the clever inventions and discoveries of men. The inventions seem natural to us, because we see their workings every day. But to the men and women of the time of Calhoun, Webster, and Clay, if they could return to the earth, these inventions and discoveries would seem more miraculous than the doings of Aladdin and his wonderful lamp of which we read with so much interest.

A SHORT STORY TO TELL

We saw in Chapter XI how steamboats, factories, railroads, telegraphy, and machinery began to change all the ways of living in the United States. The invention of new machines never stopped. More and more railroads were built, telegraph wires were stretched over all the United States. Many new factories were built, and great cities grew up around the factories. The railroads and steamboats took food and material from the farms to the cities and carried back to the farms goods from the stores and factories of the cities.

Bell invented the telephone. Marconi invented a way to send telegraph messages without wires. Then men began to study how to send telephone messages without wires, and at last they invented the radio instrument. Other men went to work to make a machine that would run on the streets and roads without horses. They made the automobile. Still others were trying to make a flying machine, and finally they invented the airplane.

Edison, the "wizard," invented the electric light and a hundred other things for the use and comfort of the people. And still the inventions are going on, making the days we live in an age of machinery. It seems that we almost live by machinery.

HOW THE MACHINE AGE AFFECTS US

1. Why is the time in which we live now often called the Machine Age?

2. Show the ways in which machinery has changed our lives. Do this by placing the headings, Before Machines, and, Since Machines, on the blackboard or on a large sheet of paper. Under these headings write the things people did before, and after machines were used. Illustrate these lists with pictures if you care to do so.

3. Report to the class what you know or can find out about Edison that has not been told in this chapter.

4. Have an Edison Roll Call. As each pupil's name is called he will give the name of one of Edison's inventions. He should be prepared with two in case his first choice has been mentioned.

5. List all the ways you can think of in which you would miss electricity if you had to be without it for the rest of your life.

Chapter XXII

THE AUTOMOBILE AND THE AIRPLANE

Henry Ford.

THE DEVELOPMENT OF RAPID TRANSPORTATION

How men learned to increase their speed. For many thousands of years men have been trying to travel faster and faster and carry heavier and heavier burdens.

The first men traveled on their own legs. They could walk and run, but nearly all of the animals around them could go faster and farther. So men began to think about how they could increase their speed. As a result of their thinking, they tamed the horse and the camel and the elephant.

The horse was more widely used than any other animal. He has been a noble friend and servant of

man. On the back of a good horse a man could travel
faster than almost any other animal. But he was not
satisfied. He wanted to go still faster, and carry
heavier loads than he could carry on the horse.

So men kept on thinking about speed. We have seen
how they built the steamboat and the locomotive. The
steamboat could go wherever the water was deep
enough, but the locomotive could travel only on the
railroads. How could men make a machine that
would be light enough to run on the country roads and
anywhere about the city streets?   *10*

THE AUTOMOBILE

The gasoline motor. The most important step toward
the making of a machine that could travel on the roads
like a wagon was the invention of the gasoline motor.

In proportion to its weight, the gasoline motor is
much stronger than the steam engine. Men then began
to ask themselves how they could attach a gasoline
engine to wheels and make it go from place to place.

The first successful automobiles were used in the
United States about 1895. In 1935 there were nearly
thirty million automobiles, trucks, motor busses, and
motor cycles in use in the United States and Canada.

A pioneer automobile manufacturer. There are many
automobile factories in the United States. They make
cars which range in price from a few hundred dollars
to several thousand dollars.

Among the makers of low priced cars, no one was
more successful than Henry Ford. Ford was born on
a farm in Michigan. He was always interested in

machinery and when he was a boy he had a workshop in his yard.

In the story of his life, which he wrote himself, Ford said that he first began thinking about automobiles when he was twelve years old. One day he and his father met a steam engine going down the road. It was heavy and clumsy and could go only a few miles an hour, but the important thing about it was that it did go. It was used to pull a threshing machine.

Ford said: "The engine had stopped to let us pass with our horses and I was off the wagon talking to the engineer before my father knew what I was up to." Later he tried to make models of this old road engine and he finally made one that would run.

"From the time I saw that road engine to today," said Ford, "my great interest has been in making an engine that would travel the roads."

Ford finished his first motor car in 1893. Since that time his factory has made more cars than any other factory in the world.

The service of the motor car. The automobile has probably done more than any other machine that was ever made to bring the different parts of our country close together. It enables people who live in the cities to go to the country for play and recreation, and it enables those who live in the country to enjoy the pleasures and advantages of the city.

In the summer when so many people take their vacations they go on long automobile trips and see different parts of our large country. They see its beautiful mountains and lakes and forests and streams. They

A very early horseless carriage.

see its splendid cities, its ranches and farms, its churches and schools. They are proud of the beauty and greatness of our country. The automobile helps to educate us and to make us happier and more useful and more patriotic citizens.

THE AIRPLANE

Man's longing to fly. Men have always wanted to fly. The Greeks had a story three thousand years ago about a man who made his son a pair of wings and warned him not to fly too near the sun. But the boy was so happy that he forgot his father's warning. He flew higher and higher until the heat of the sun melted the wax that held the feathers on the wings and he fell into the sea.

The beginning of the airplane. Many men have worked to make the airplane, and, like the automobile, it owes its success to the invention of the gasoline engine.

Professor Samuel P. Langley was the first to invent a flying machine that would fly. He was born in Massachusetts, and was at one time a professor in Harvard University. When he made his flying machine, he was working for the government at Washington.

Langley's first machine weighed twenty-six pounds and the wings measured about thirteen feet from tip to tip. His machine made two flights in 1896. Each trip was about half a mile.

After proving that his machine would fly, Langley set to work to make a machine large enough to carry a man. His first experiment with the larger machine failed and he could never get enough money to make another trial. The work that he did, however, helped others to succeed later.

The Wright brothers. Orville and Wilbur Wright were brothers. They had a bicycle shop in Dayton, Ohio. When Langley's machine made its successful flight in 1896 they were already interested in flying. They used all their spare time trying to make a glider that would carry a man.

They succeeded with the glider and then they took up the task of making a machine with an engine that would furnish enough power to lift, by means of the tilted plane, the machine and a man. In 1903 they made their first flight in an air machine.

The Wrights had made their experiments at Kitty Hawk, North Carolina, and this first machine has been named the *Kitty Hawk.*

The development of the airplane. The Wright's kept on with their experiments, and many others took up the work, all trying to improve the airplane and make it safer and faster.

In 1914 the World War began. The army commanders found airplanes useful for flying over the enemy's lines, making photographs, gathering information, and directing artillery fire. Many improvements were made in the machines, and flyers of all nations became very skillful.

When the war ended, planes began to be widely used for carrying passengers and mail. So rapid was the improvement in motors and construction that before the year 1931 flyers had crossed the Atlantic and Pacific oceans many times, and several planes had flown around the world.

Lindbergh's work for aviation. While the World War was going on Charles A. Lindbergh was a high school student in Minnesota. He made his first airplane flight in 1922. During the next three years he studied in flying schools at Lincoln, Nebraska, and San Antonio, Texas.

In 1927 Lindbergh, in the *Spirit of St. Louis,* flew across the continent from California to New York. Ten days later he started alone, with a bottle of water and a few sandwiches, and landed in Paris. He was the first man to cross the Atlantic in an airplane alone.

The flight to Paris made Lindbergh famous. He

was entertained by the governments of France, Belgium, and England. On his return to the United States President Coolidge welcomed him at Washington.

Lindbergh next made a tour of the larger cities of the United States in his *Spirit of St. Louis* for the purpose of stimulating interest in flying.

He next visited Mexico, Central America, and the West India Islands. In 1931 he and his wife flew across the northern part of the Pacific Ocean to Japan, and then went on from Japan to China. A great part of China was flooded by overflowing rivers, and thousands of Chinese people were dying of starvation and disease. Lindbergh joined in the relief work and used his plane to carry food and medicine to the sufferers.

Lindbergh's career did much to stimulate the interest of the people of the United States in aviation.

THE AIRPLANE AT THE NORTH AND SOUTH POLE

Polar exploration. The first man to reach the North Pole was an American, Commander Robert E. Peary, of the United States Navy. He traveled with dog sleds and arrived at the Pole in 1909. The second explorer to reach the North Pole was also an American, Richard E. Byrd, and like Peary, he too was a commander in the navy. Byrd traveled by airplane and flew over the Pole in 1926.

Byrd was the third explorer to reach the South Pole. The first to get there was Roald Amundsen, a Norwegian, and the second was Robert F. Scott, an Englishman. Amundsen and Scott traveled with dogs

Charles A. Lindbergh and his airplane the "Spirit of St. Louis" in
which he flew alone across the ocean from New York to Paris in
May, 1927. He made this flight of 3,610 miles in 33½ hours.

and sleds. Byrd made his exploration again in an airplane.

The Story of Admiral Byrd. Richard Evelyn Byrd
was born in Virginia in 1888. While he was a student
in the Naval Academy at Annapolis he fell in the
gymnasium and broke his ankle. The bones did not
heal, and after a short service at sea he was retired
from active service on account of his weak ankle. Fortunately no serious result followed.

During the World War he was called to service in
the Navy Department. He said that his work here

was to move men from station to station and papers
from basket to basket.

Byrd did not like office work. He wanted to learn
to fly. Finally he got permission to take a vacation
and go to a flying school in Florida. After taking
lessons for six hours, he made his first flight alone.
The next year he was made commander of the United
States air forces in Canada.

Flying over the North Pole. After the war was over,
Commander Byrd remained in the air service. In
1925 Congress furnished him ships and airplanes and
allowed him to lead an expedition to the Arctic Ocean.
He had worked out a plan and had determined to fly
to the North Pole.

Find the man who had not used an oar before.

This expedition failed to reach the Pole, but Byrd was not discouraged. He returned to the United States and raised enough money from his friends and supporters to go north again the next year.

"We were going this time," he said, "on our own hook." All the men who sailed with him were volunteers. His ship landed him on the island of Spitzbergen in the Arctic Ocean, about six hundred miles from the Pole. The airship, the *Josephine Ford,* was lifted from the boat and let down among the floating chunks of ice to be towed ashore on a raft. While the men were putting the wings on the ship a great wind came and almost carried it away. When they had got the raft ready "a big iceberg came galloping in with the tide," threatening to crush not only the raft but the steamship as well.

Byrd's men met the iceberg with dynamite and blasted it to pieces. At last the airplane was on the raft and was started toward the shore amid the floating ice. Many of the men had never handled an oar, some rowed the wrong way, and an engineer "used his oar backwards all the way to land." But every man did his part cheerfully.

The troubles were not ended when the airplane was finally on land. In fact, it was not on land, but on snow and ice. In order to take off from the snow the giant plane was equipped with snowshoes or skis instead of wheels, and no one knew how a great ship like the *Josephine Ford* would behave on snowshoes. What happened was that the skis were broken like paper, not once but twice. The third time they were made from the oars of the boats, the last wood that the men could get.

Two men were to go on the trip, Commander Byrd and Floyd Bennett. Neither of them had slept for thirty-six hours, but this did not bother them. All was ready, the runway had been iced and leveled, and the motors warmed. Byrd wrote: "A few handclasps from our comrades and we set our faces toward our goal and the midnight sun. With a total load of nearly ten thousand pounds we raced down the runway. The rough snow ahead loomed dangerously near but we never reached it. We were off for our great adventure!"

At two minutes past nine o'clock, May 9, 1926, they were at the Pole. And there everything became topsy-turvy. They flew around the Pole in a few minutes. In flying over the Pole on a straight line they were going north one minute and south the next without changing the direction of flight. At the Pole, however one turns he is always facing south.

Byrd flies across the Atlantic. The next year Commander Byrd flew across the Atlantic, most of the way in a storm. For hours Byrd and his three companions could see neither the sky above nor the water below. They reached Paris with the storm still raging and in such a fog that they could not see the lights of the landing field. Their gasoline was about out, and something had to be done. They turned the plane back towards the sea, and came down in the water not very far from the shore.

On this trip Byrd was sworn in as the first trans-

Commander Byrd starts for the South Pole.

Atlantic air mail pilot, and carried the first bag of air mail from the United States to France.

Flying over the South Pole. Not satisfied with having reached the North Pole in an airplane, Commander Byrd decided to go also to the South Pole. After nearly a year of preparation, he set out for the South Pole in 1928. This expedition was far more dangerous than any he had before undertaken. First, there are no good ports near the South Pole where ships can land; and, second, it is much colder, with more snow and ice, there than at the North Pole.

Byrd took with him four planes, the *Floyd Bennett,* named for his faithful companion on the North Pole flight, the *Stars and Stripes,* the *Virginia,* and a giant monoplane. He established his home camp on the ice at a place the men named Little America. It was twenty-four hundred miles from the nearest human dwelling and nearly eight hundred miles from the Pole.

Here the forty men of the expedition unloaded the hundred Eskimo dogs, the four planes, and a supply of food for two years. In ten days they had built an airport, and exploring parties were going out to map and photograph the land.

Just as our spring was coming here winter was closing down on Little America. And what a winter! On July 4 the thermometer showed sixty-seven degrees below zero.

The men had built houses in the ice. They had plenty of food and warm fur clothing. Each day they received radio programs from the far away world. Sometimes they sent messages to the outside world.

The hundred Eskimo dogs, when not mushing over the snow to lay a base line of food and gasoline towards the Pole, were housed in caverns of ice. They were chained in boxes to keep them from fighting, and each day were taken out for exercise.

In November, as the southern spring approached, Byrd completed his preparations for the dash to the Pole. On Thanksgiving Day he set out with three companions in the *Floyd Bennett* "on a voyage never before attempted by man."

To reach the Pole the ship had to travel nearly eight hundred miles. Over the first four hundred and fifty miles Byrd had laid bases of food and fuel, so that if his ship was forced down he could repair it and start again.

Just beyond the last base the plane had to rise to a

height of twelve thousand feet to get over the Queen Maude Mountains. It was heavily loaded, and its strength was taxed to the limit. At times it was barely three hundred feet above the ice-covered peaks. Half the food supply was thrown over to lighten the load. But the barrier was crossed and the happy explorers were on the last stage of their journey.

After more than eight hours' flight the instruments showed that the ship was at the Pole. Then they flew around in a wide circle to be sure to pass all around the Pole. In nineteen hours from the time that they started the explorers were safe back at Little America.

In 1933 Admiral Byrd led a second expedition to Little America to make scientific studies and observations.

A SHORT STORY TO TELL

For many thousands of years men have tried to increase their speed. At first they could go no faster than they could run. Then they tamed the horse, and for a long, long time they could go no faster than the fastest horse could run.

About a hundred years ago, as we have seen, the steamboat and the railroad came into use. The next step was the automobile and the airplane. Both of these machines were made possible by the invention of the gasoline engine.

In 1935 there were nearly thirty million motor vehicles in use in the United States and Canada. More automobiles are made and used in the United States than in all the other countries of the world put together.

The first flying machine was flown in the United States in 1896. In 1903 the Wright brothers made a machine that would carry a man. Eleven years later the World War began and all the armies made use of machines and flyers to gather information and direct the firing of their big guns.

After the war was over planes began to be used for many things—to carry passengers, mail, and freight, and to explore distant regions. Several flyers have flown around the world, and Admiral Byrd has flown to both the North and the South Poles.

SHOWING HOW TRAVEL IS IMPROVED

1. Make a picture chart which will show how the automobile serves us, or one showing the uses of the airplane.

2. Make a poster that will encourage people to use airplanes for travel.

3. Make a Roll of Honor on which you will write the names of the persons who have helped to improve travel on land and in the air. Under each name write briefly what the person did.

HUNT AND FIND

4. In chapter xxii find the sentences which answer the following questions:

What was the most important step in the development of the auto?

What gave Ford his first interest in building autos?

Who was the first trans-Atlantic air-mail pilot?

316- 322

13

Chapter XXIII
OUR NATION LEARNS TO PLAY

IN THE DAYS OF LITTLE PLAY

Living out of doors. When our great-grandfathers were young there were only five or six large cities in the United States. Nearly all of our people lived in the country or in little towns. They did not need parks and playgrounds and gymnasiums because their homes were in the open country and all who could work had so many things to do that they probably thought little about special outings or exercise.

In the pioneer home everybody worked. In the winter, besides caring for the farm animals, the men chopped down trees to clear the land for a new field. Sometimes they hauled logs to a nearby stream to be floated in the spring to a saw-mill and made into lumber. Spring was the time for sowing and planting. In summer the hay and early grains were gathered, and in fall harvesting was finished and fruits and vegetables were put away for the winter.

The burning of the brush, waste wood, and stumps on the cut-over ground was also a late summer job for men and boys.

The wife and mother in a pioneer farm home was the busiest woman in the world — cooking, washing dishes and clothing, keeping the house clean and tidy, making and mending clothing, spinning and knitting, making soap, often planting and caring for the garden, and, greatest of all, raising a family of healthy, wholesome, useful boys and girls.

As the children of a family became old enough, they became active partners in all kinds of home work and responsibility.

Boys cut and carried in the wood for the stove and fire-place, carried in water from the well-spring or pump, brought the cows from the pasture and milked them, planted corn, potatoes and beans, raked the hay by hand and helped to haul and stack it, cut and husked corn, dug and picked up potatoes, and did chores of all kinds.

The girls were equally busy. They learned to help to keep the house clean and tidy, to prepare food and cook it, to knit and sew and make clothing for themselves and other members of the family, to make butter and cheese. Girls commonly fed the chickens, ducks, geese and turkeys, gathered the eggs and helped to care for the broods of all the young fowl. They gathered and helped to preserve fruits, wild as well as tame. When in a family girls were numerous and boys few, the girls often helped Father in the fields; raking hay or driving a team in some of the lighter kinds of team work.

Another reason for the lack of games was this: There were not so many people in our country then as there are now. Most of them lived on farms, several miles from their nearest neighbors. There were few schools to bring the children together. So it happened that children of different families could not often get together to play, even when their parents were willing for them to have games.

Pioneer life did not prevent play. It would be a grave mistake to suggest that there was no play in pioneer farm life. The school always allowed some time for play and children chose and adapted games to their needs. The farm home was a good place for hide and seek, pom pom pull-away, and simple ball games. The streams and lakes provided swimming and skating. Boys found real sport in fishing and hunting. Both boys and girls found pleasure in horse-back riding, if only to the store or post-office. There were barn-raisings, husking bees, and apple-paring bees, usually followed by a dance. The one fiddler at these parties was as good as a full orchestra for the occasion.

13

THE PEOPLE TURN TO GAMES

The growth of cities and schools. Gradually conditions of living for many people changed and plans for play had to change. Great cities grew up, with factories and stores and tall office buildings, and with solid blocks of apartments and houses. People could no longer get to the open country by walking a little distance from their front doors. Miles of pavement took the place of shady roads and grassy pastures. Hundreds of thousands of young men and young women left the farms to work in the cities.

As the cities grew larger, the men who governed them began to try to bring back into them a little of the country. They made parks, into which people might go for picnics.

At the same time that the cities were growing large the public free school system began. So many children came together in the schools that it was necessary for them to have playgrounds.

After a while people began to think about games and play in a new way. They saw that children, and grown people too, could do better work when they took a little time off from their daily tasks to rest and play. Teachers began to see that children may learn some of the most valuable lessons of life on the playground: to be honest and fair in their games; to be good-humored and keep on playing when the game went against them; to think quickly and act promptly. They saw that good habits formed on the playground would help boys and girls grow into good citizens.

. **The rise of games.** The most popular game in the
United States for boys and men is baseball. Boys play
baseball wherever they can get together and find a little space. They play in the country, in parks, and in
vacant city lots. Many cities have paid teams to play
against the teams of other cities. Schools and colleges
have teams to play against other similar teams. And
the boys on one street play against the boys who live
on another street.

As a game that calls for the best a player has, the fine
thing about baseball is that it can be played during so
many years of one's life; maybe seven to fifty-seven.

Next to baseball, the game that the American people

seem to like best is football. This game, however, is played most by college and high school teams. People go to see the games because they like to see keen contests of that kind; quick thinking, swift running and dodging, daring blocking and tackling as well as skillful kicking. To all this is added the joy of being a part of gay, excited crowds, waving banners and rooting for their teams.

Basketball, tennis, and track games are popular sports, but they are not so exciting as baseball and football and fewer people go to see them played. Hundreds of thousands of men and women are playing golf on courses as attractive as good public parks.

A sportsman becomes President. Theodore Roosevelt was a great sportsman. He liked to see games played and he liked to play them himself. When he was a young man he lived on a ranch, as we have already seen, and hunted and rode horseback. When he became President of the United States he built a tennis court near the White House and made it a practice to play two or three times a week. He kept up his riding. He played basketball and handball with his children. And he liked to wrestle and box in the gymnasium.

President Roosevelt believed that people should live as much as possible out of doors. He said that all children ought to live in the country or in towns and cities so small that they could easily get to the woods.

Some old-fashioned people still believed that it was undignified and improper for the President of the United States to spend so much time in games. They thought he ought to stay in his office and spend all his time thinking about how to run the government. But there were fortunately many others who began to say: "Well, if the President plays games and teaches his children to play, games must be all right." So more and more people turned to games and sports and out-door amusements.

PARKS AND PLAYGROUNDS

National Parks. The men who run our government know that it is important for the people to have beautiful playgrounds. So, on the land owned by the government, our Presidents and senators and congressmen have set aside a great number of national parks and national forests. They will not sell the land in these parks and forests; and many thousands of people visit them every year.

Anyone who wishes can go into the national parks and forests and stay as long as he pleases. He can camp in a tent or a cabin or live in a hotel as comfortable as any in the largest city.

One who likes the beauty of nature finds in the national parks some of the most delightful scenery in the world. There are snow-capped mountains, and gushing hot springs that throw water high into the air. There are beautiful waterfalls, and the oldest and largest trees in the world. There are cave homes of cliff-dwelling Indians who disappeared before Columbus discovered America. There are canyons and gorges, and a river with banks a mile high painted in all the colors of the rainbow.

One who enjoys studying wild animals can see herds of deer and elk and buffalo. And the bears are so tame in parts of the national parks that they come into the camps and eat all the sugar and cakes they can find about the place.

Travelers and campers must follow the rules. They must leave their camping places clean. They must put out their camp fires. They must be careful not to drop burning matches or cigarettes or cigars. They must not cut down the trees nor shoot at the birds or other animals.

State parks. Our states, too, are beginning to set aside land for parks and forests like those of the national government. They furnish safe homes for birds and harmless animals, and are open and free to campers and travelers who are willing to obey the rules.

City parks and playgrounds. Hundreds of thousands of people drive through the national parks and forests every year. But many millions who live in the cities cannot go so far. For them there must be parks nearer home. So the men and women who govern our cities are giving more and more attention to city parks. They want to put a pleasant playground within reach of every child.

The large city parks provide games and amusements for people of all ages. One may see a dozen games as he strolls along. There are baseball and football fields and tennis courts and golf courses. There are places for flying kites. There are lakes and pools for swimming, paths for horseback riding, and grassy lawns for picnics and other parties.

GAMES FOR EVERYBODY

Getting rid of the "bleacher players." There is a story
of an Indian who for the first time saw a man riding a
bicycle. He grunted and said: "White man lazy; run
sitting down." Too many boys and girls used to play
their games sitting down. They sat in the grandstand
or stood on the side lines and cheered the school team.

It is a fine thing to have a school team. It is a fine
thing to play on the team. But our teachers and doctors know that the best thing of all is for every boy
and girl to take part in games of their own. They have
learned the truth of the saying, "all work and no play
makes Jack a dull boy."

A SHORT STORY TO TELL

In the early years of our nation, the people did not believe in games as much as they do now. They thought it a waste of time to play. We know now that games and play are an important part of the education of boys and girls. Play in the open air makes them healthy and strong. Games teach them how to be good citizens when they become men and women, and that is the purpose of all education. They learn to be fair to their playmates. They learn to be "good losers" and "modest winners." They learn to resent bullying and to despise cheating.

Because we know the value of play, the men and women whom we elect to manage our government have made parks and playgrounds in many parts of the country. We have national parks, state parks, and city parks and playgrounds. They are all intended to make us healthier, happier and better citizens.

LOCATING OUR PLAYGROUNDS

1. Find out all you can about our national parks. Locate several of these on a map of the United States.

2. See if you can find out about your state parks. Make a map of your state and show where the parks are located.

3. Make a map which will show the part of your town necessary to locate your home and the nearest playground.

4. The class might make a map of your entire city or town and locate all the parks and playgrounds.

Chapter XXIV

THE UNITED STATES TODAY

Many Alaska Eskimos live in little houses, often called igloos, made of hard-packed snow.

THE LANDS THAT WE OWN

The home land. The home territory of the United States is made up of forty-eight states and the District of Columbia, which contains the beautiful city of Washington, the home of our government. The United States reaches from Canada in the north to Mexico in the south, from the Atlantic Ocean in the east to the Pacific in the west. More than half of the land in North America that is comfortable for white people to live in is in the United States.

It is a fortunate land. It is blessed with a pleasant climate. It contains timber, iron, coal, oil, gold, silver, and nearly all the minerals that its people need. It raises every kind of food needed by mankind. It produces the materials for the busy factories that make our clothing and furniture and tools and machinery.

Each of the forty-eight states has its own government to manage its affairs and to look after its own people. The federal government at Washington keeps all the states at peace with one another, and looks after matters too large and important for single states to manage.

Colonial territory. Besides its home land the United States has other territories far away. It is often said that the sun never sets on the British Empire, because its land is scattered in all parts of the earth. That statement is almost true now of the United States.

The territory of Alaska. Alaska is the oldest and largest of these far-off lands belonging to the United States. Congress bought it from Russia in 1867 for seven million dollars. It is one-fifth as large as the United States. On account of its cold climate, however, it has very few people. In 1930 it had nearly sixty thousand people, about half of whom were whites and the rest Eskimo Indians. All of them together would make only one little city in the United States.

Alaska is valuable for its gold, silver, and copper; for its great forests; for its furs; and for its salmon fisheries. The value of the salmon caught in Alaskan waters in a single year is more than five times what the United States paid for the whole country.

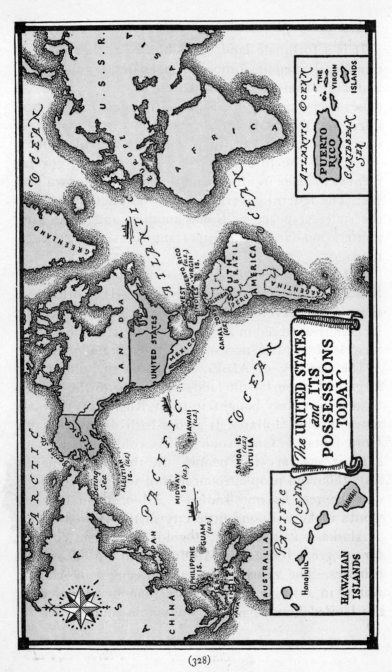

The UNITED STATES and ITS POSSESSIONS TODAY

PUERTO RICO

THE VIRGIN ISLANDS

Atlantic Ocean

CARIBBEAN SEA

HAWAIIAN ISLANDS

HAWAII

Honolulu

Pacific Ocean

ARCTIC OCEAN

GREENLAND

U. S. S. R.

AFRICA

EUROPE

CANADA

UNITED STATES

MEXICO

ATLANTIC OCEAN

WEST INDIES

PUERTO RICO (U.S.)

VIRGIN IS.

COLOMBIA

CANAL ZONE (U.S.)

PERU

SOUTH AMERICA

BRAZIL

ARGENTINA

PACIFIC OCEAN

ALASKA (U.S.)

Bering Sea

ALEUTIAN IS. (U.S.)

HAWAII (U.S.)

MIDWAY IS. (U.S.)

SAMOA IS. (U.S.)

TUTUILA

GUAM (U.S.)

PHILIPPINE IS.

JAPAN

CHINA

EAST INDIES

JAVA

AUSTRALIA

It is always summer weather in the Philippine Islands. Many people there live in grass-roofed houses.

Alaska is too cold for cattle, but some years ago our government sent twelve hundred reindeer to the territory for the use of the Eskimos. This herd has increased to nearly half a million, and reindeer meat has been shipped from Alaska to the United States for food. It is much like beef.

The people of Alaska elect their own legislature, as we do in the states, and they send a representative to sit in Congress in Washington. But their governor is appointed by the President of the United States.

The islands belonging to the United States. Besides some small islands that it owns in the Atlantic and Pacific oceans, the United States has two important island colonies. These are the Hawaiian Islands and Puerto Rico.

Hawaii.   Hawaii is a group of islands in the Pacific Ocean some twenty-five hundred miles west of California. Hawaii was added to the United States in 1898, when the people who lived there asked the United States to take the islands. The government is like that of Alaska. The people elect their own legislature and send a representative to sit in Congress in Washington. The President of the United States appoints their governor.

The climate of Hawaii is pleasant, and remains about the same all the year round. The chief business of the islands is making sugar and raising fruit. The largest canning factory in the world is in Hawaii. It cans nothing but pineapples.

Puerto Rico.   Puerto Rico is a little island of the West Indies, east of Cuba. It has more than a million and a half people. Its main crops are sugar, tobacco, coffee, and fruits. The people elect their own legislature to make the laws for the island, but the governor is appointed by the President of the United States.

Puerto Rico was discovered by Columbus on his second voyage in 1493. It came into the possession of the United States in 1898 as the result of a treaty with Spain. In the short time since the United States took possession, the people have made more progress in health, wealth, and education than they made in all the centuries that Spain owned them.

The Philippine Islands.   As a result of war between the United States and Spain in 1898, the United States obtained possession of the Philippine Islands. During the next thirty-five years, the government of the islands was controlled by President and Congress, though, for a part of that time, the Filipinos had a legislature which made their own laws. A strong desire for independence grew up among the Filipino people, and in 1934 our Congress passed a law recognizing the independence of the islands. But, the law provided that the United States should continue to exercise some supervision over the Philippine government until 1948.

The Panama Canal Zone. The United States also controls the Panama Canal. The Canal Zone is a strip of land ten miles wide and about fifty miles long. Through it runs the canal that connects the Atlantic and Pacific oceans. The United States does not own the Canal Zone, but rents it from the Republic of Panama. It pays Panama two hundred and fifty thousand dollars a year for the Canal Zone, and has the right to continue renting it for the same price forever.

THE WELFARE AND HAPPINESS OF THE PEOPLE

Wealth. The United States is the richest nation in the world. Its business men and bankers have carried on business and lent money in every land. In that way American money has been used not only for the enjoyment of Americans, but also to improve farms, to build factories and railroads, and to beautify cities in many other countries far away. It has helped to better the health and increase the comfort and happiness of people throughout the earth.

The prosperity of the people. The United States is not only the richest nation, but for many years its working people have received higher wages and lived more comfortably than those of any other country.

Congress and the state legislatures have passed many laws to protect the health and safety of working people. There are, for example, laws which limit the length of the working day; laws forbidding the employment of children; and laws which compel employers to insure their employes against death or injury by accident.

Public education. Our government is a government by the people. In order to elect honest and capable officers, the voters must be educated. Education teaches us to think clearly and honestly. It shows us our duty to our fellow-citizens and to our country.

Each of the forty-eight states has a system of public schools. In some states the public schools begin with the kindergarten and end with the state university. The public schools are free, and some states provide free textbooks. Most of the states have laws saying that children must go to school a number of months each year.

FRANKLIN D. ROOSEVELT'S WAR ON THE DEPRESSION

The presidency. It would be a mistake, however, to suppose that the United States has never suffered from hard times. The truth of the matter is that we have had many periods of hard times which we call panics, or depressions. One of the most serious panics that our people have ever suffered began in 1929.

Franklin D. Roosevelt became President in March, 1933. He had served as governor of New York, and had had much experience in dealing with difficult problems of government. Under his direction, Congress passed many laws for the purpose of ending the depression, and giving people confidence in the future.

The purpose of these laws was good. Mr. Roosevelt wished to make all of the people more prosperous and happy than they had ever been before. It takes a long time in a nation as large as ours for the full effects of some important laws to be felt, so that we do not know yet how much good or ill the laws may cause.

A GLANCE BACKWARD AND FORWARD

The end of the story. We have now reached the end of our story, the story of the United States of America.

The story began with a vast, beautiful wild land of waving forests, wide plains, lofty mountains, rippling lakes, and streams winding down to the sea, all swarming with wild game, fish, and fowl, but empty of people except scattered tribes of red men.

The story ends with the United States today, a land in which only the mountains appear unchanged. Steamboats cover the waters; smiling farms, bustling towns, and splendid cities have taken the place of forests and plains. And nearly a hundred and thirty million people live happily where a handful of red savages used to chase buffalo, elk, and deer.

Railroads and paved highways cross the country like lines on a checker-board. Engines draw long freight trains and fine passenger trains with the speed of the wind. Trucks, busses, and automobiles flash along the highways. Airplanes roar overhead. Wires hum with telegraph and telephone messages. The air throbs, if we could only feel it, with wireless and radio messages.

For the present the story is ended. But history never ends. A new chapter begins tomorrow, and the future belongs to us. Shall we do as well with the future as our forefathers did with the past? We ought to try to do at least a little better.

A SHORT STORY TO TELL

The lands of the United States are made up of forty-eight states and many territories. Alaska, in the Far North, is the oldest territory. The other territories are islands in the Atlantic and the Pacific oceans. Most of these island territories came to the United States from Spain after the Spanish-American War.

MAP WORK

1. On a map of the world point out the possessions of the United States. Tell from whom we got the territory and what its chief products are.

A BOOKLET TO MAKE

2. Choose one of the possessions of the United States and find other information about it. Make a booklet in which you write a story about the territory and include pictures from magazines, or of your own drawing.

WHY WE ARE RICH

3. Write a paragraph or two in which you tell why the United States is the richest nation in the world.

DICTIONARY—INDEX

ă=băt   ê=êvent   ĭ=ĭll   ô=ôbey
à=àmericà   ĕ=mĕt   ō=nōte   ōō=lōōp
ē=shē   ī=tīme   ŏ=nŏt   ŭ=ŭs